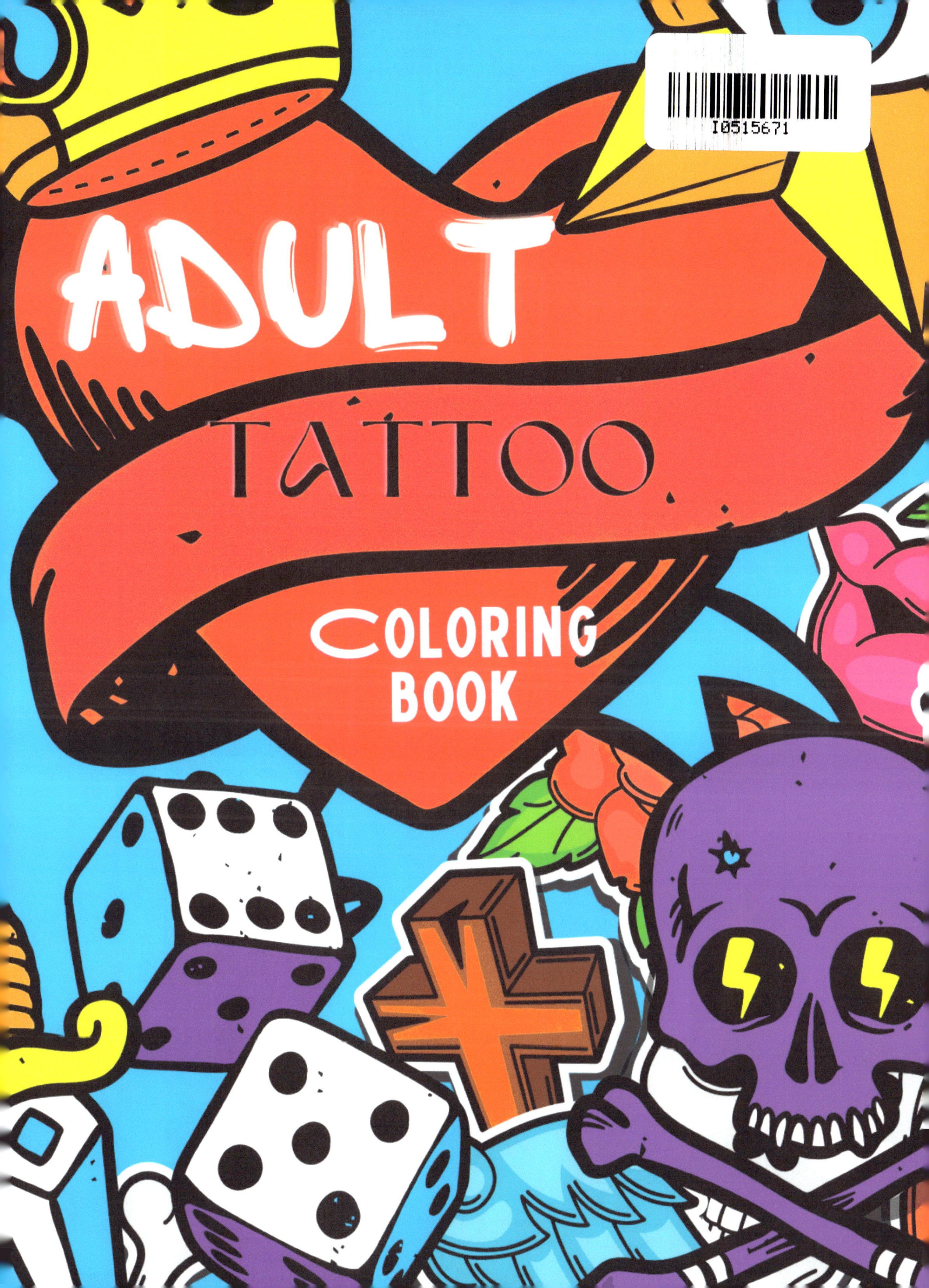
ADULT
TATTOO
COLORING
BOOK

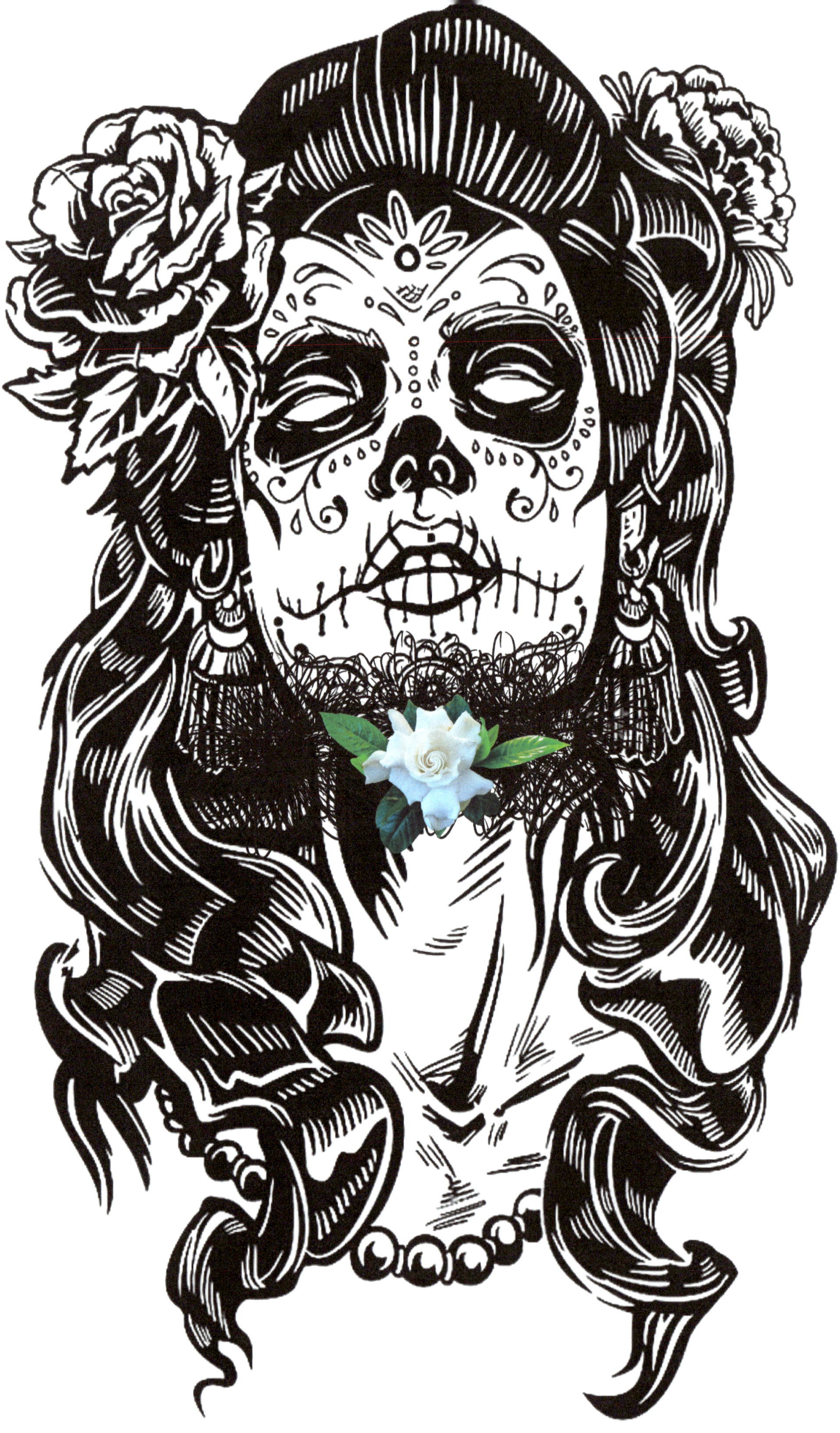

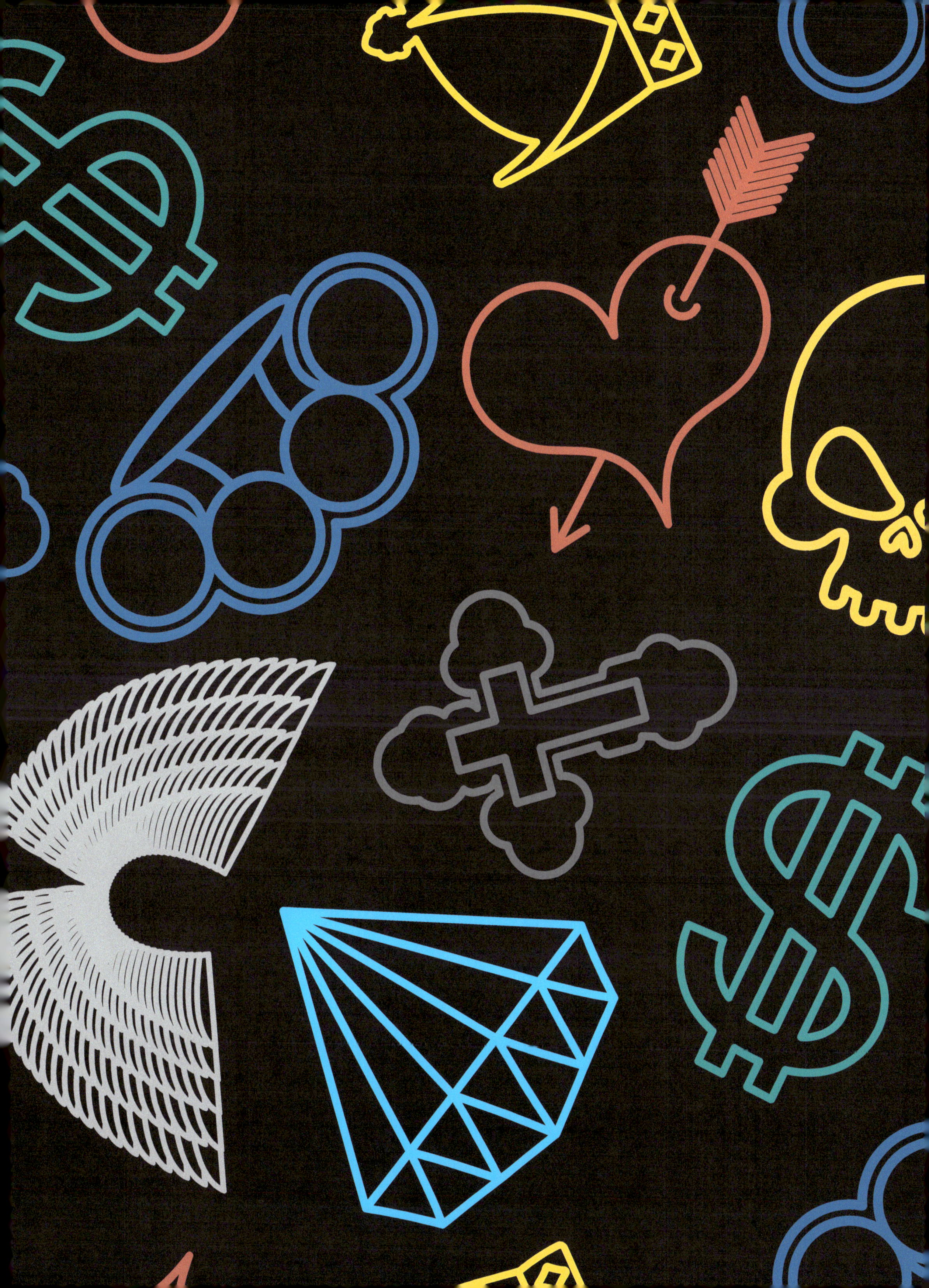

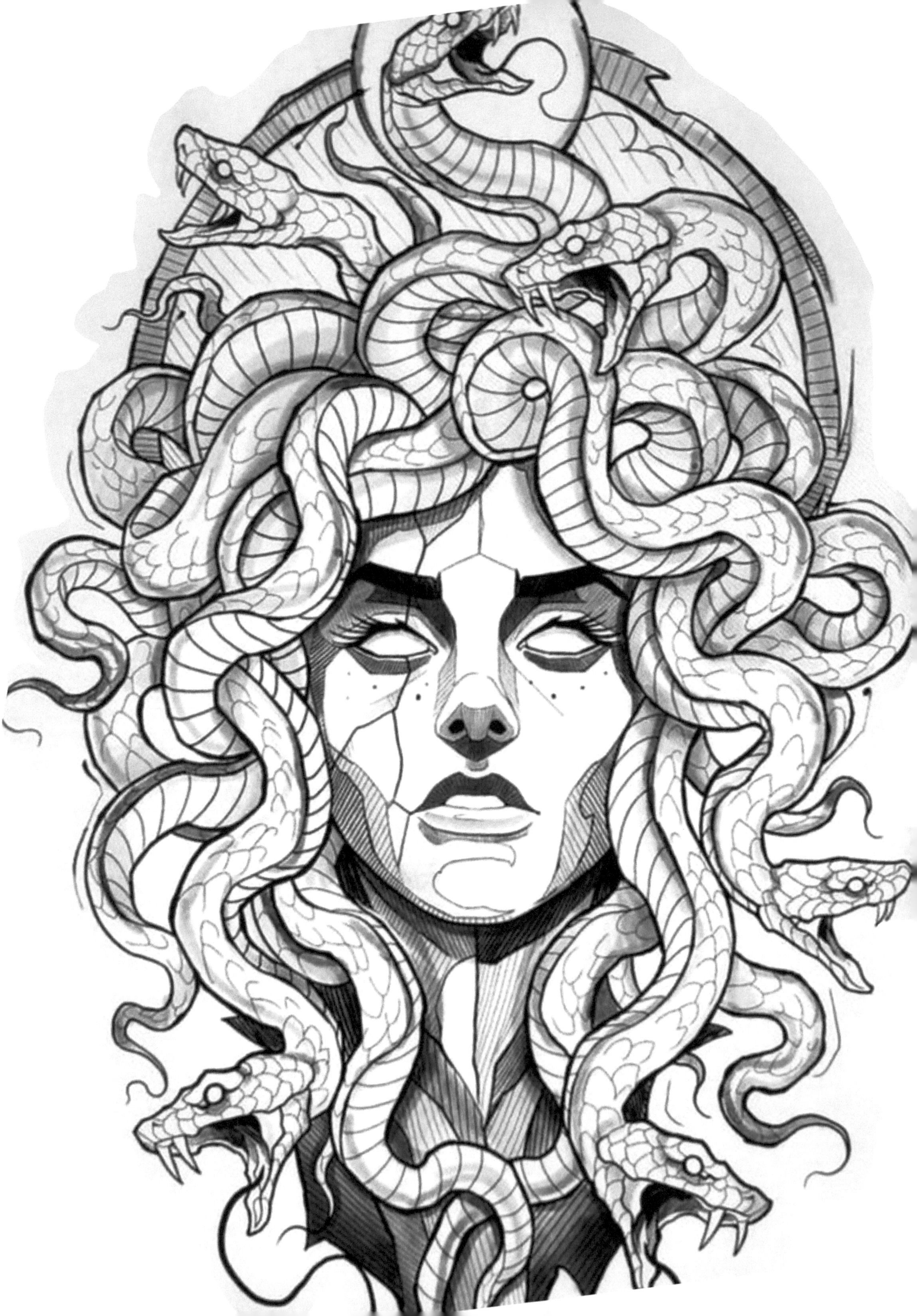

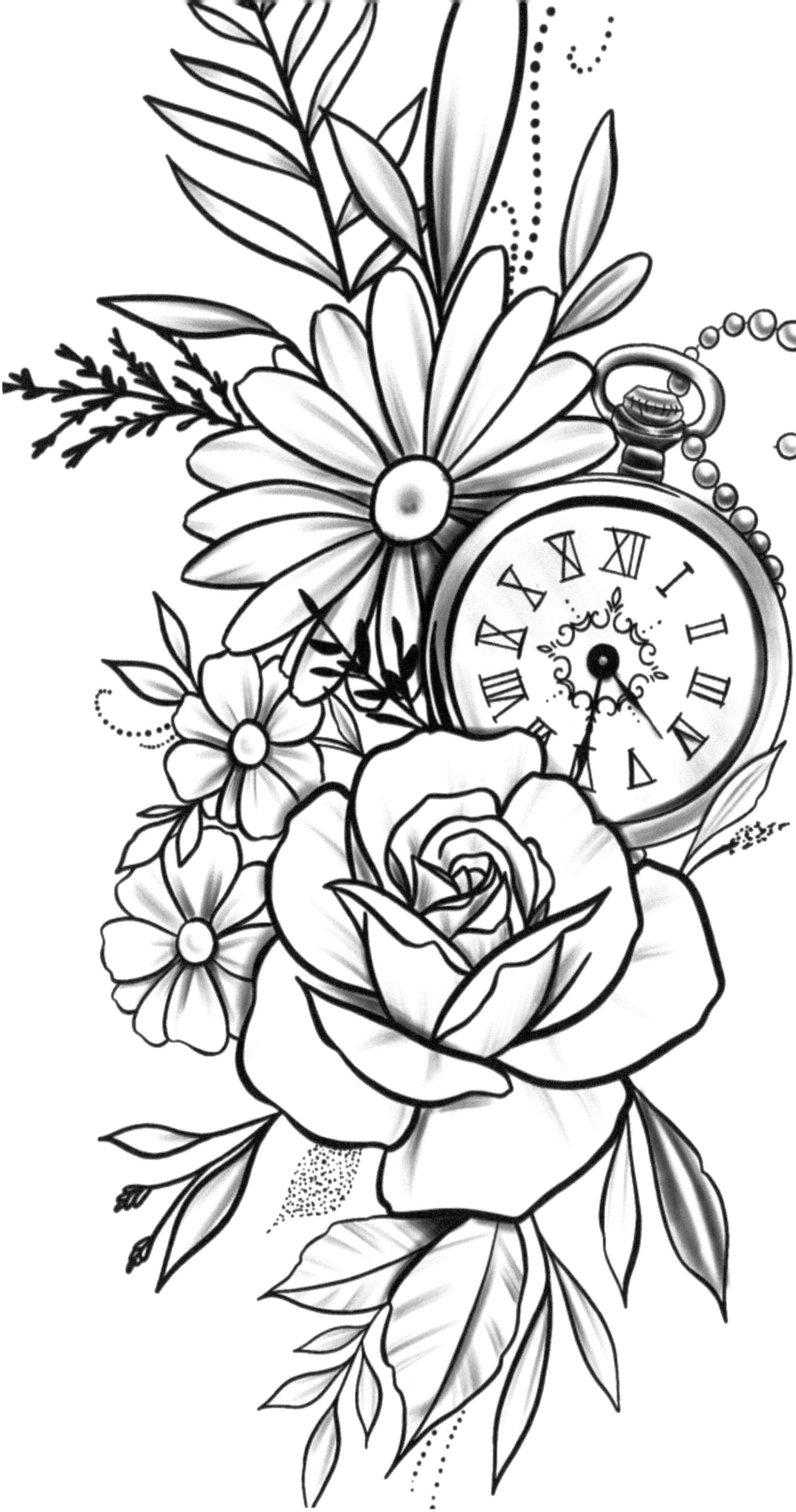

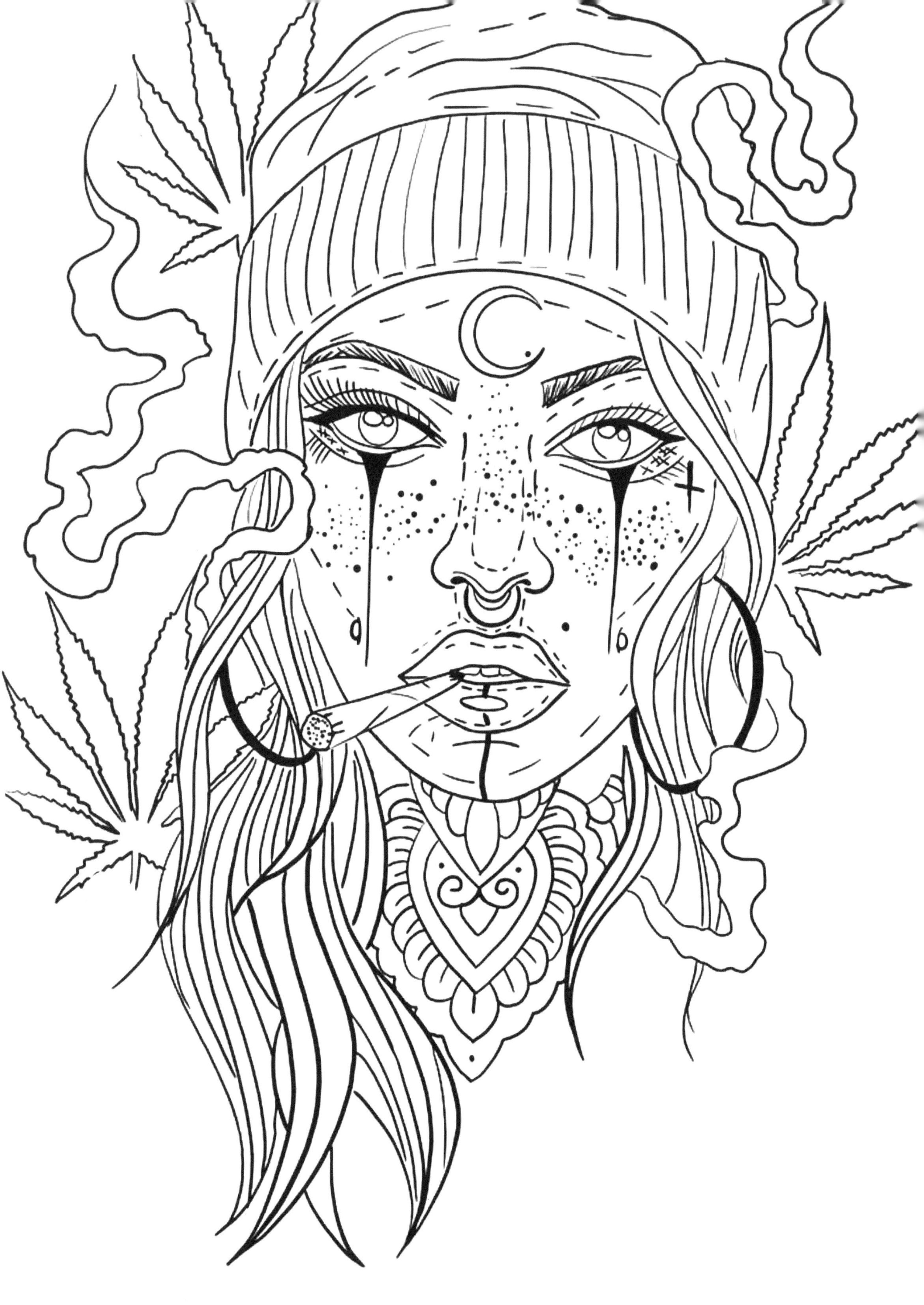

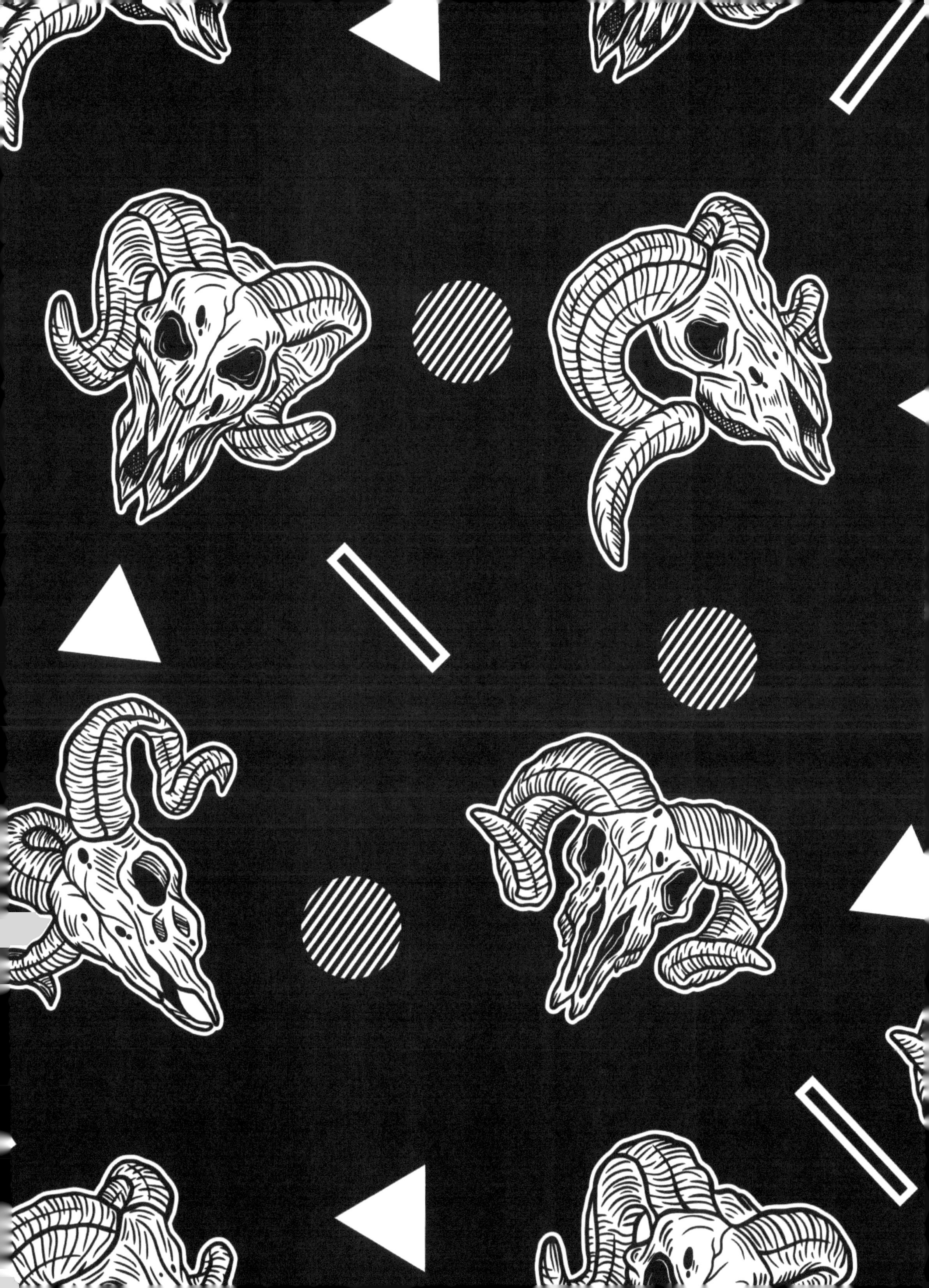

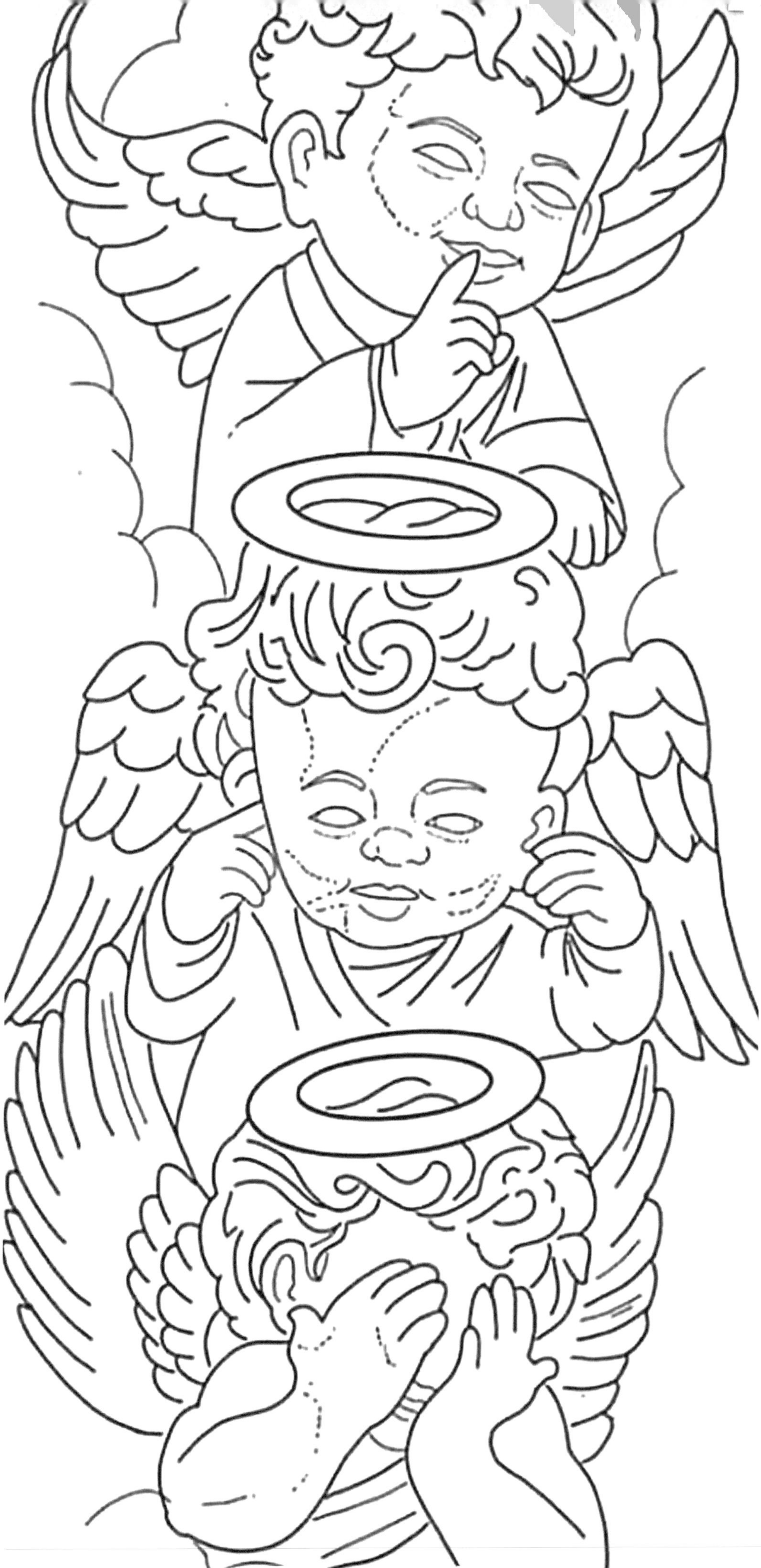

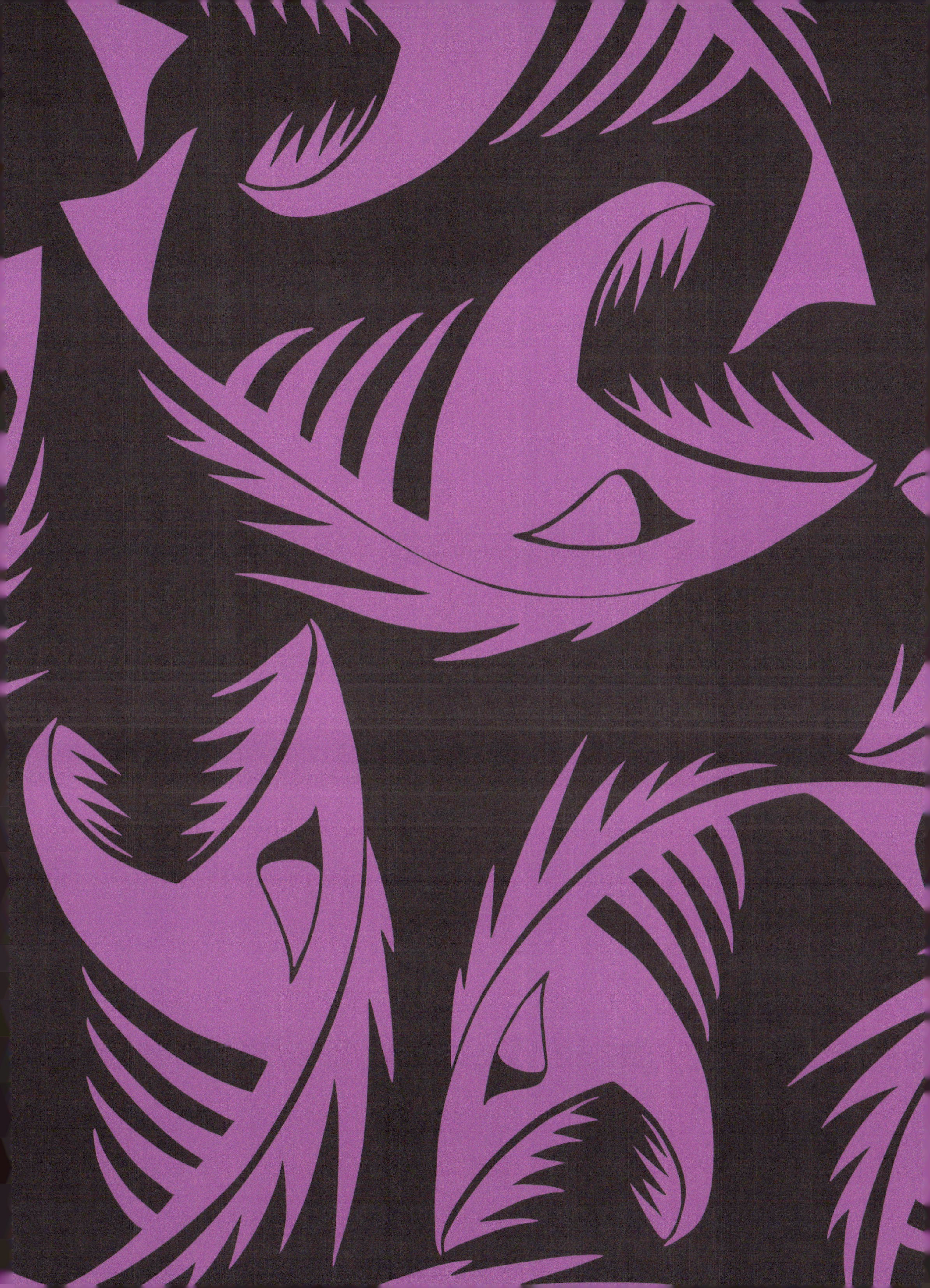

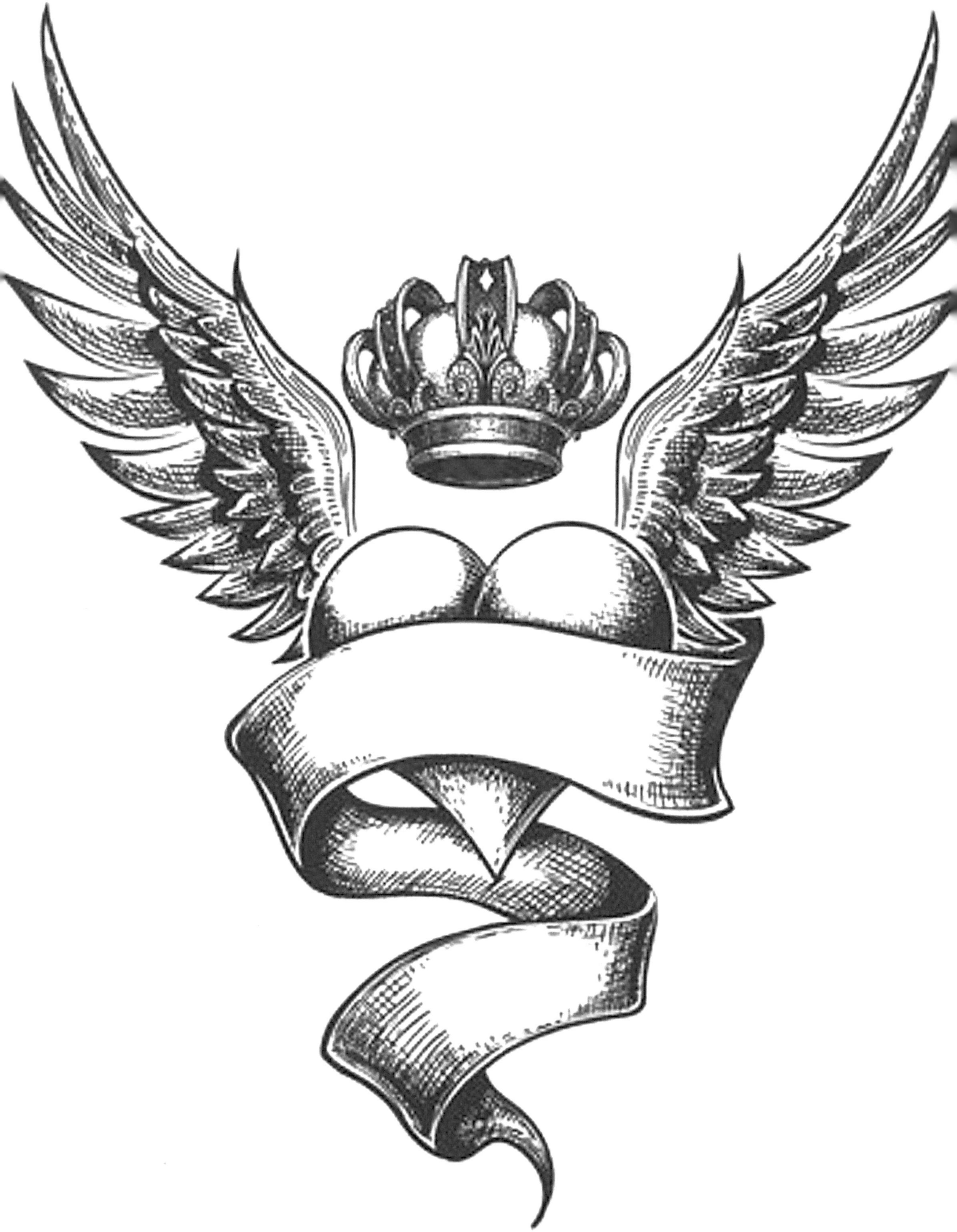

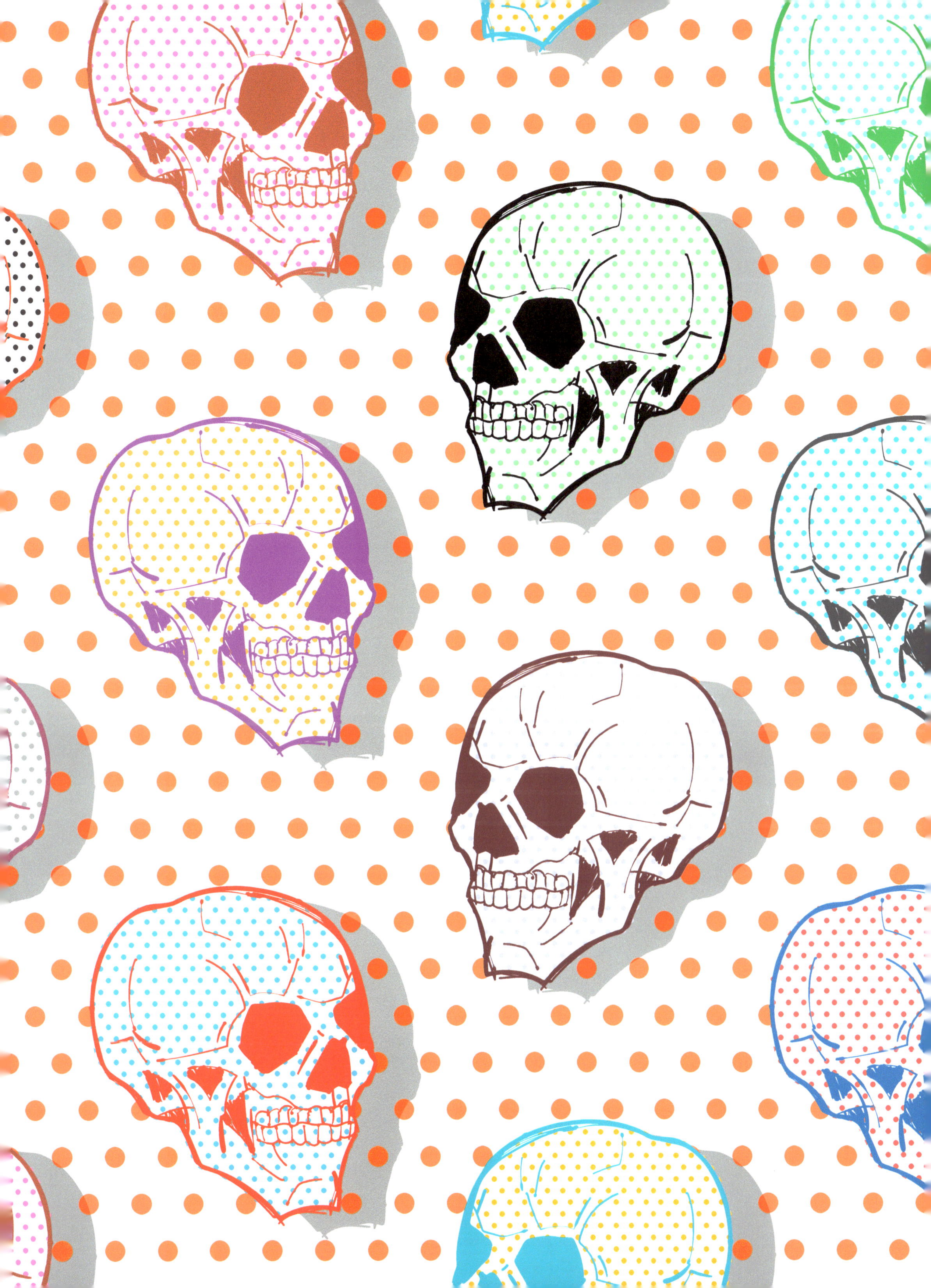

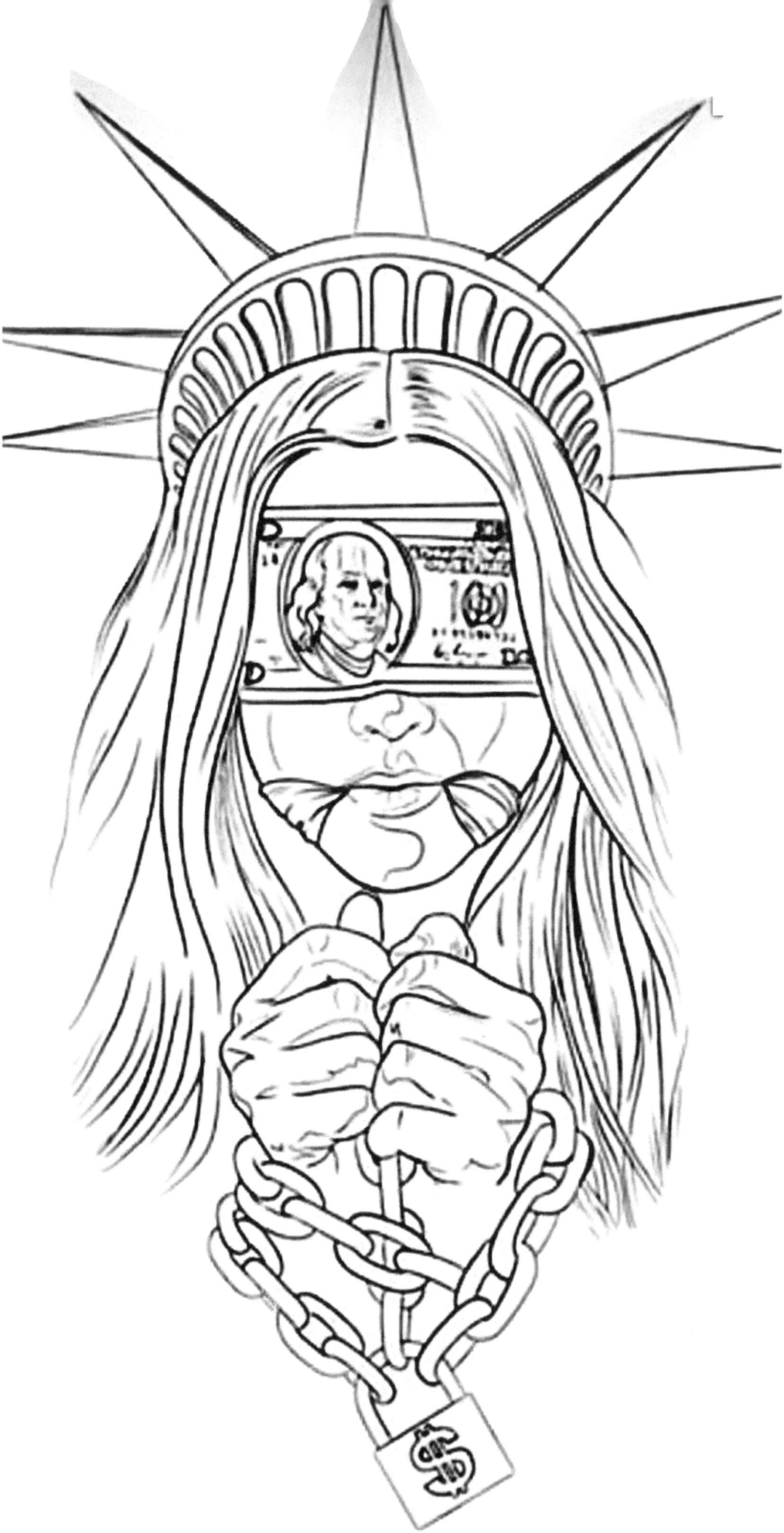

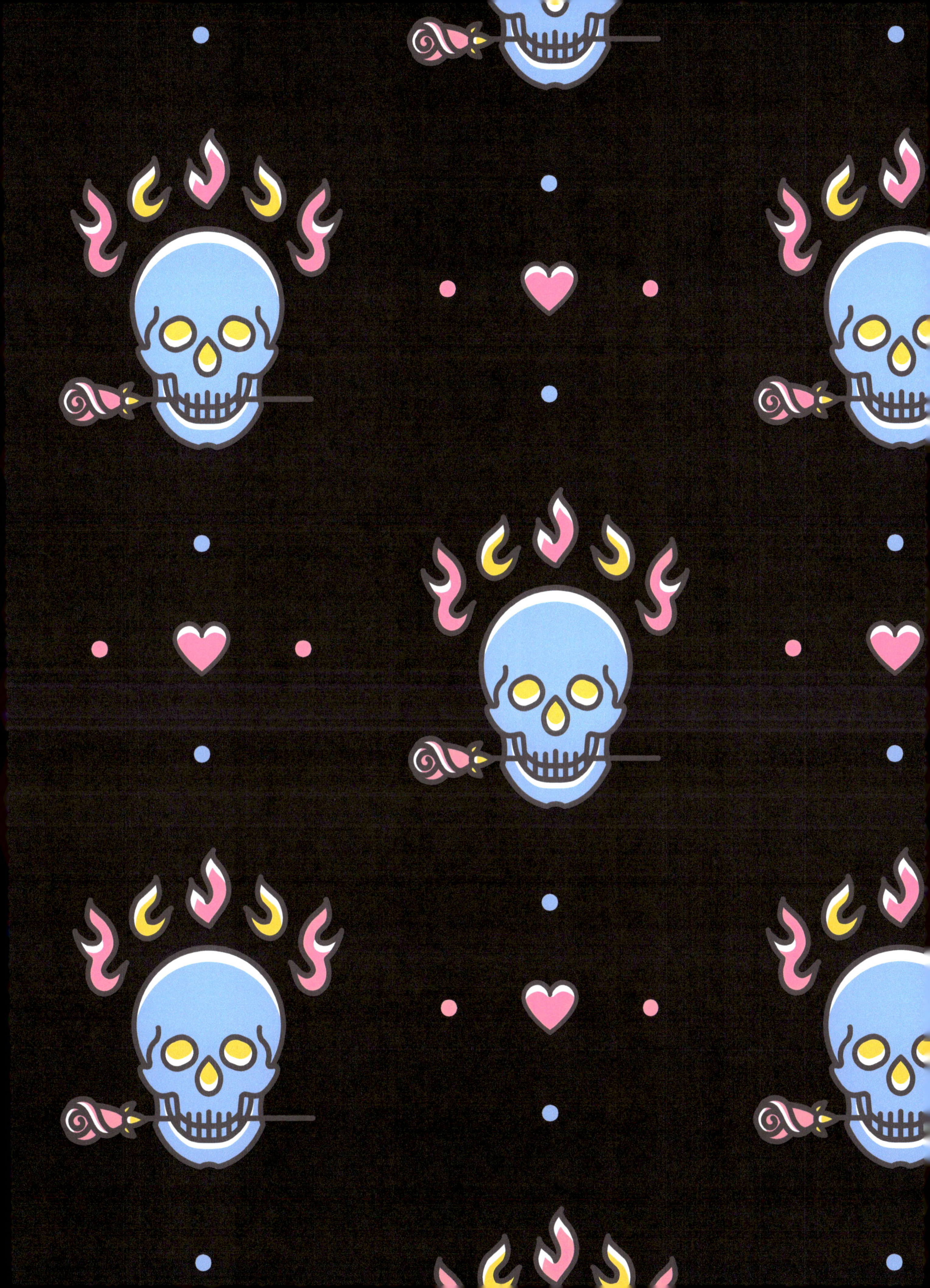

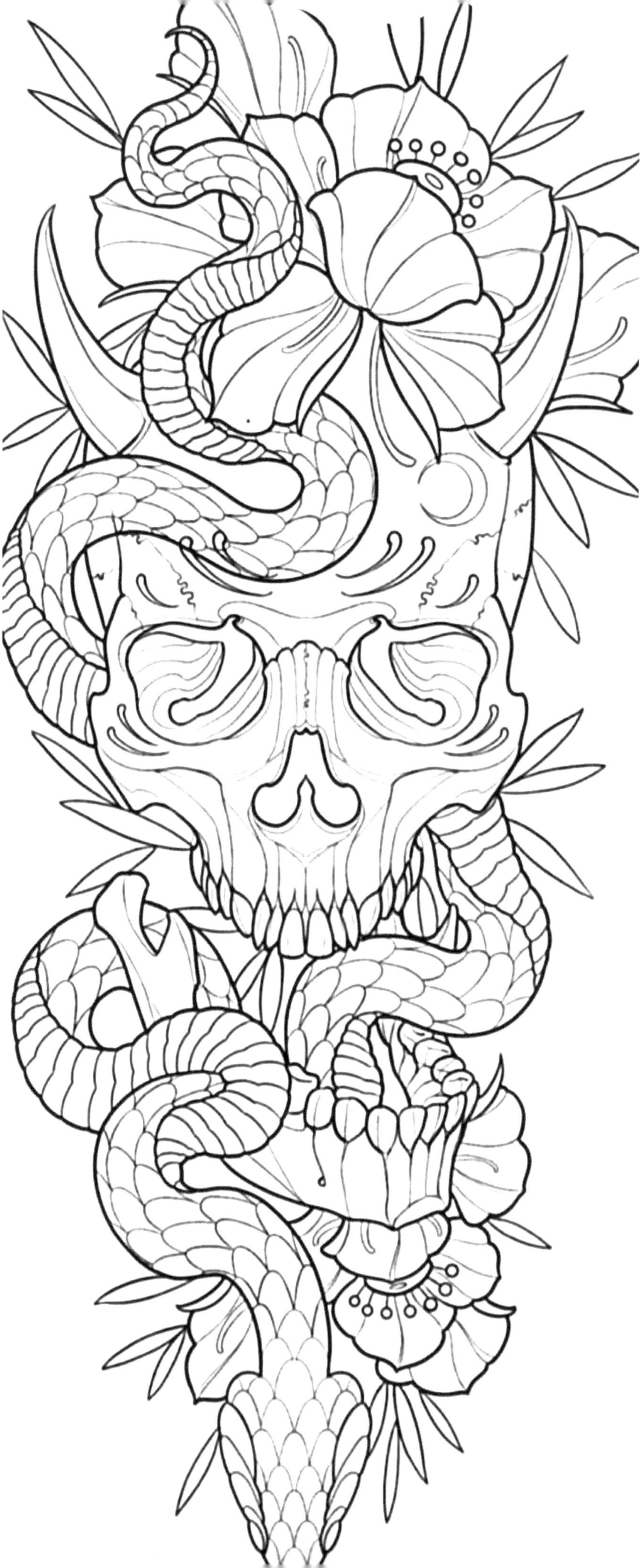

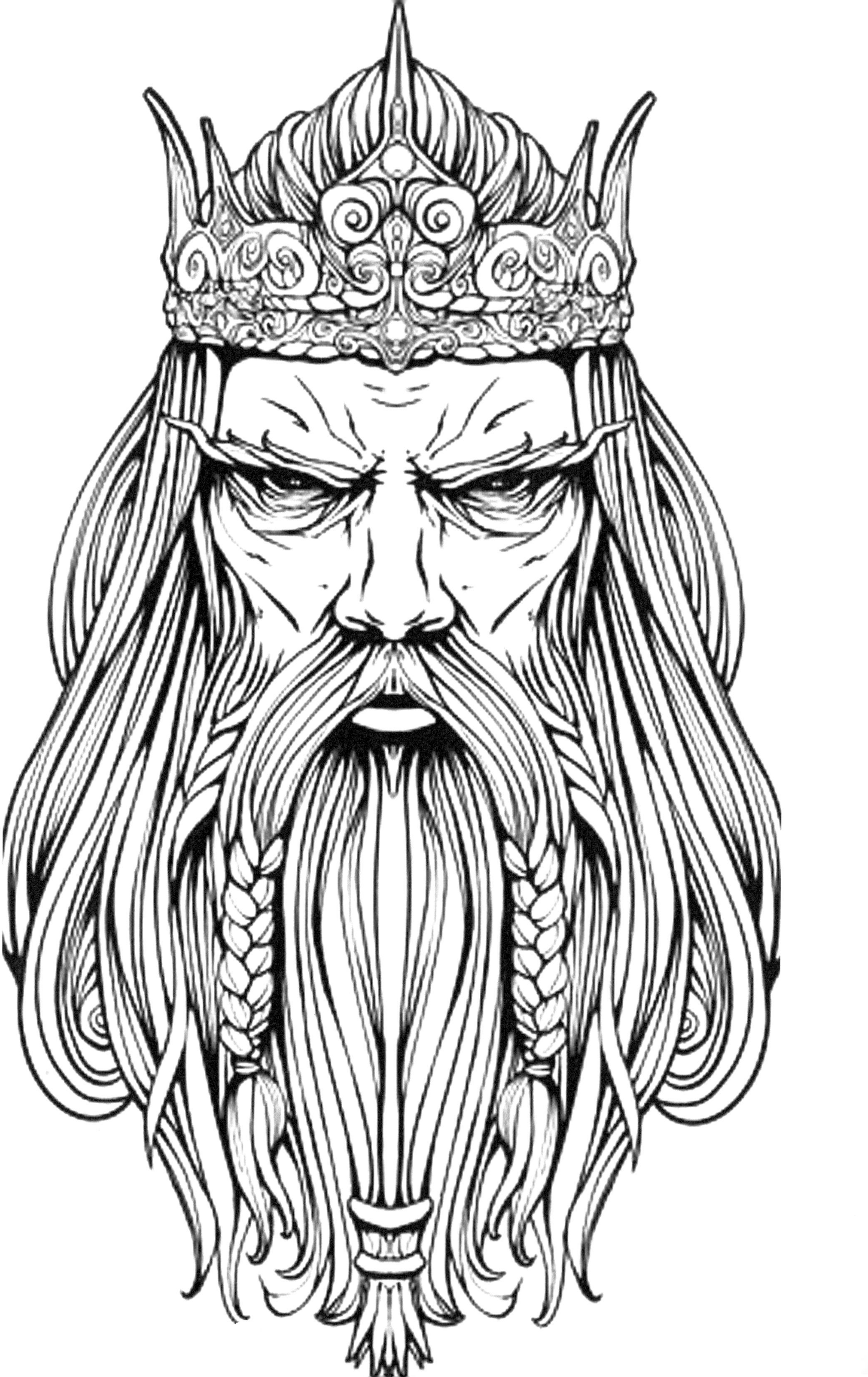

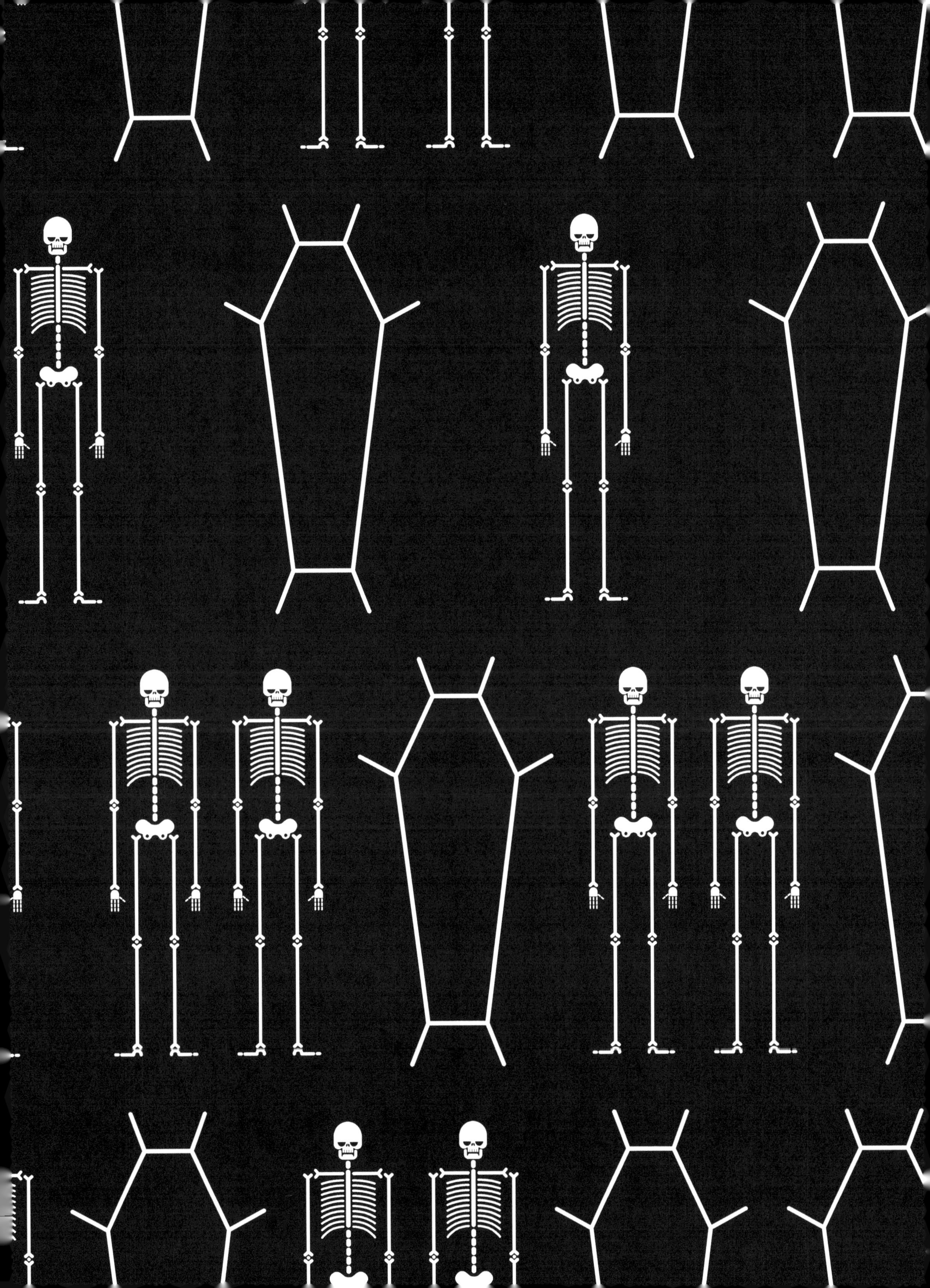

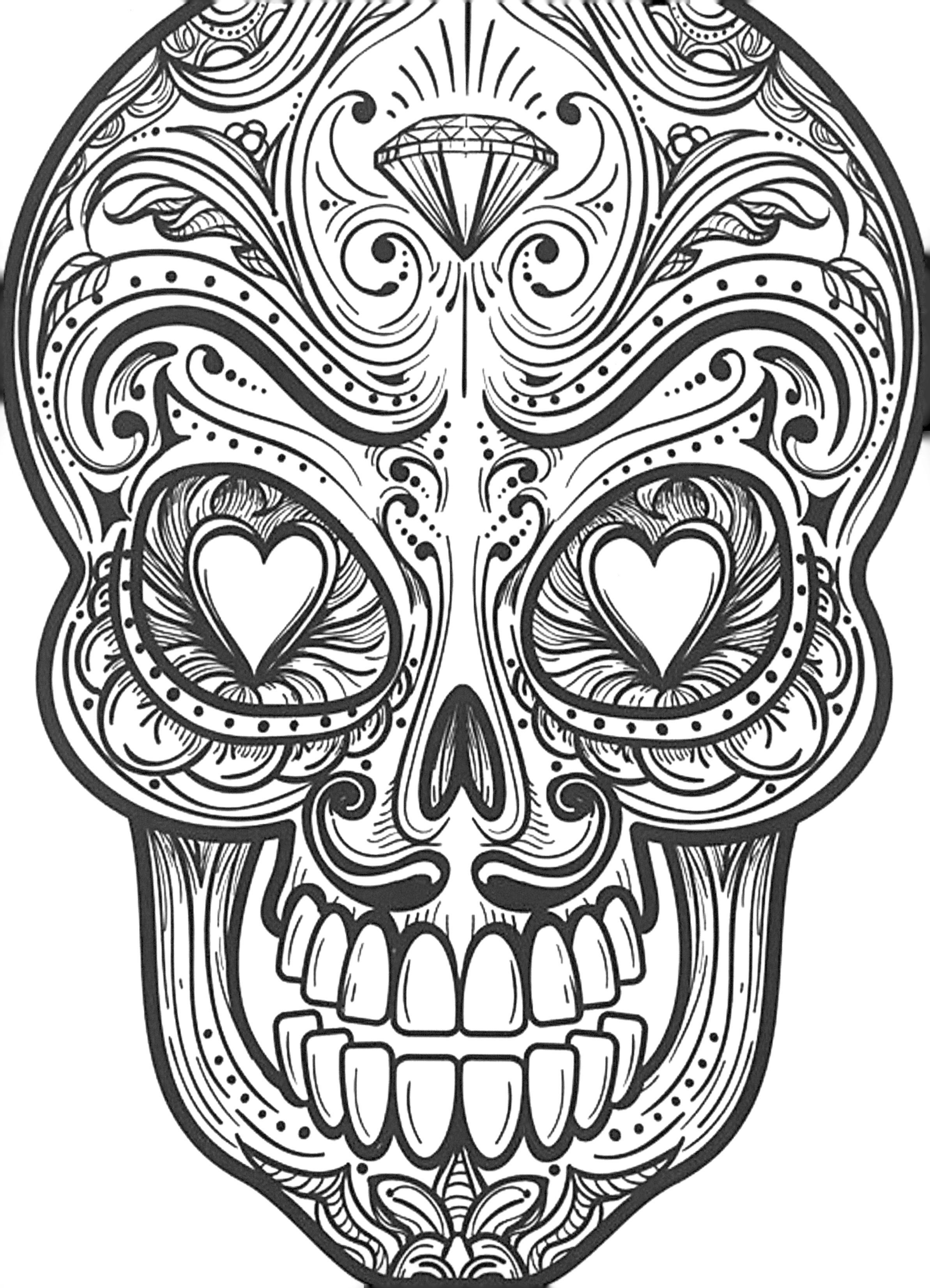

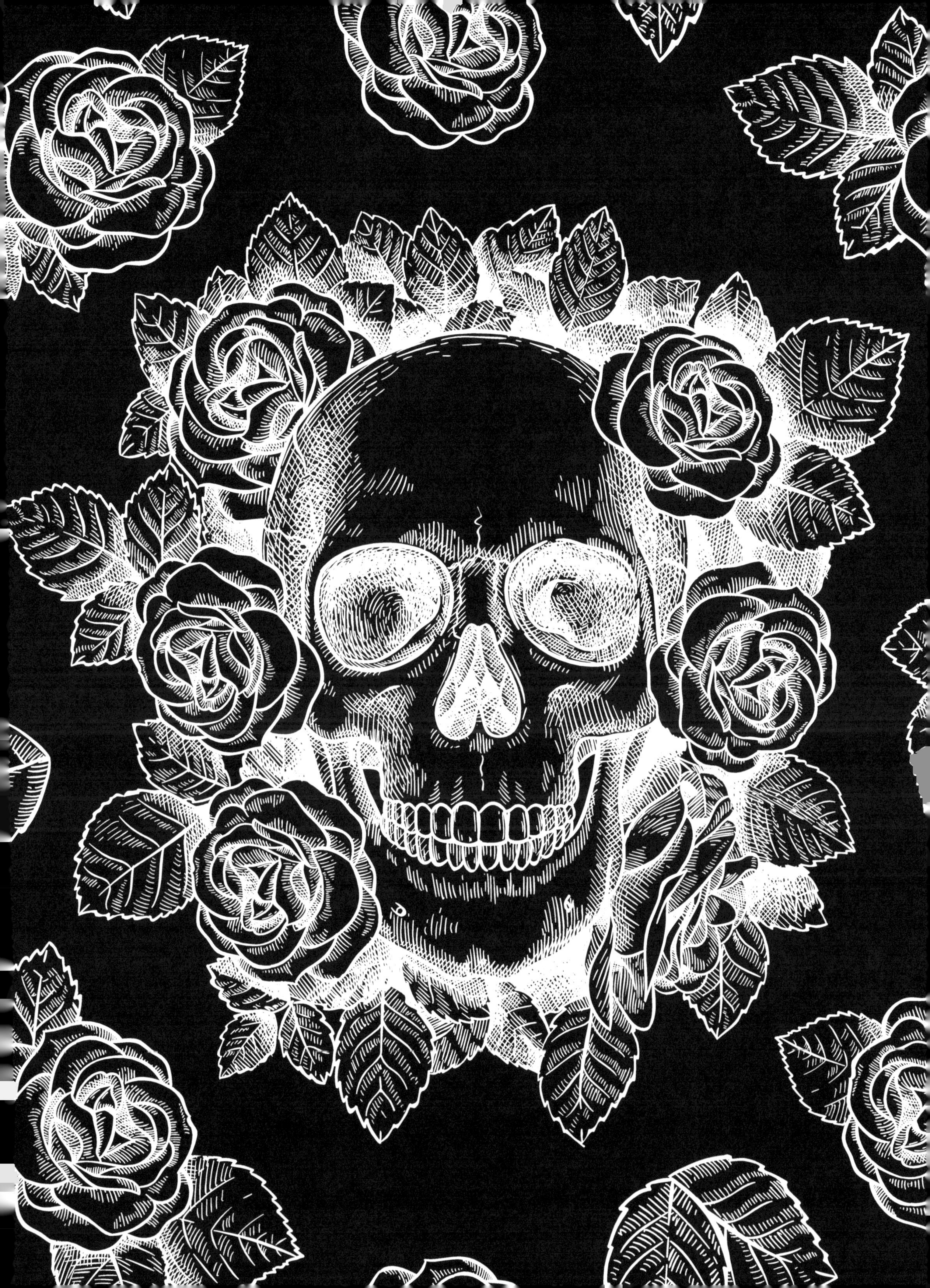

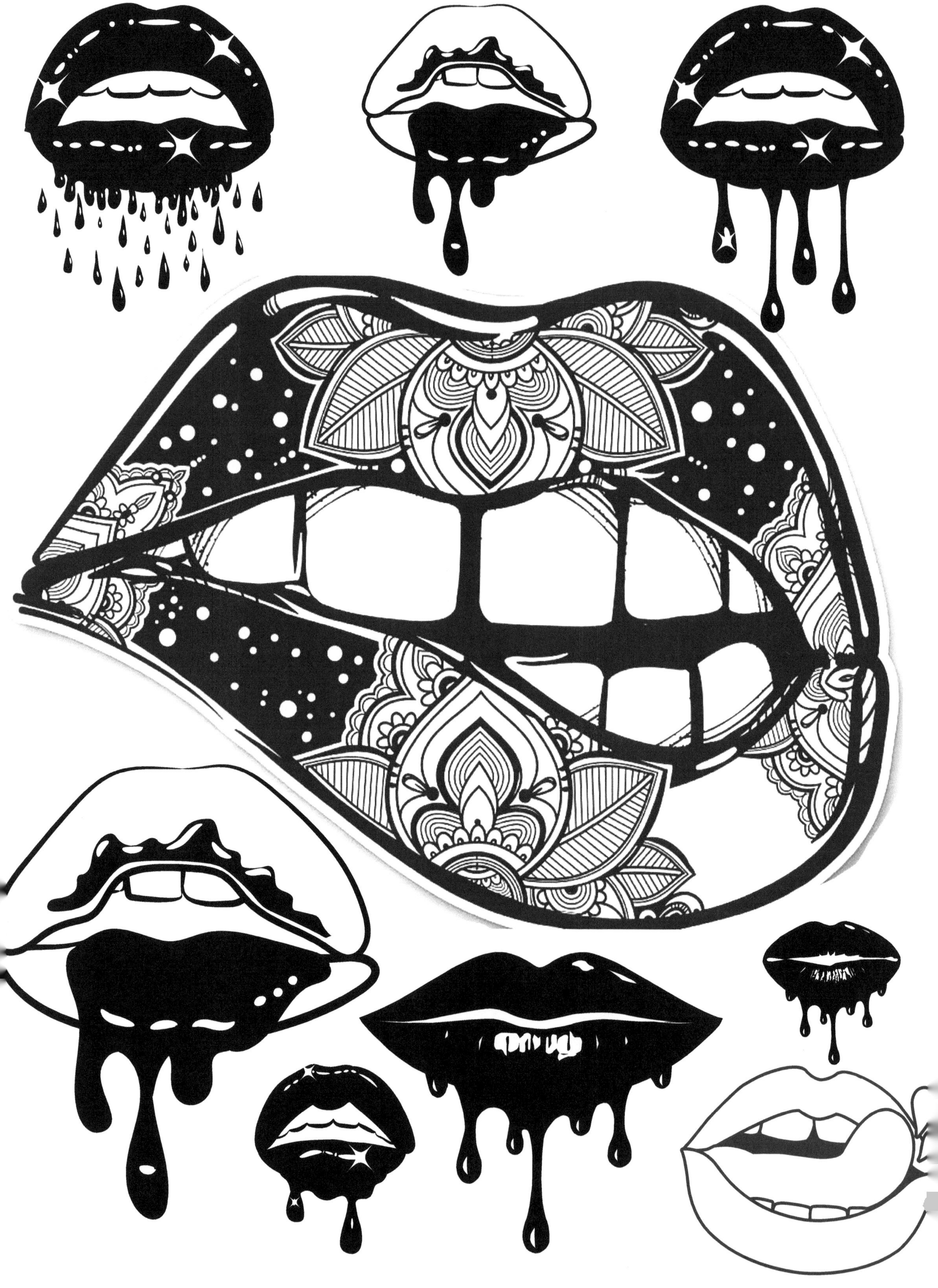

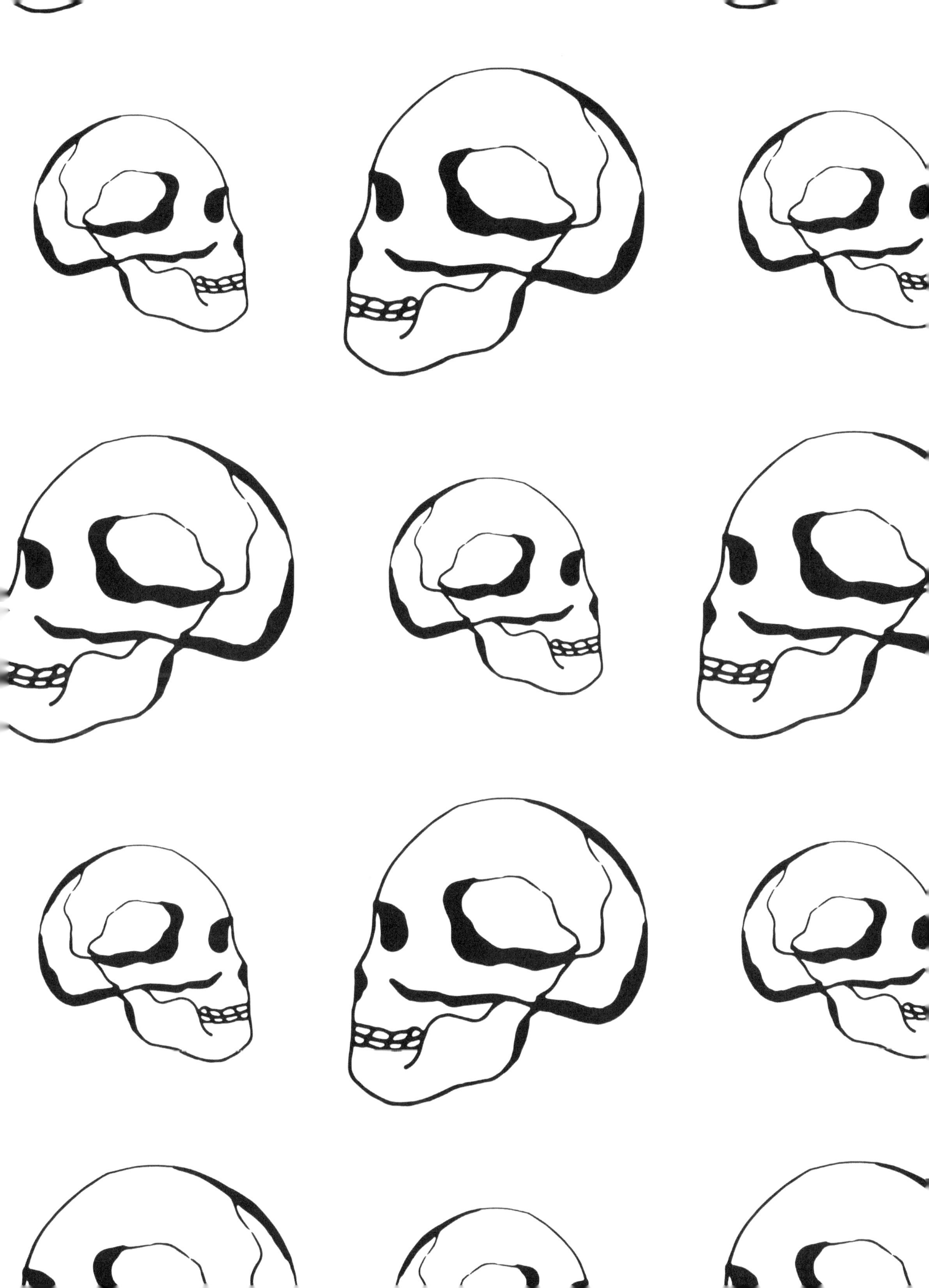

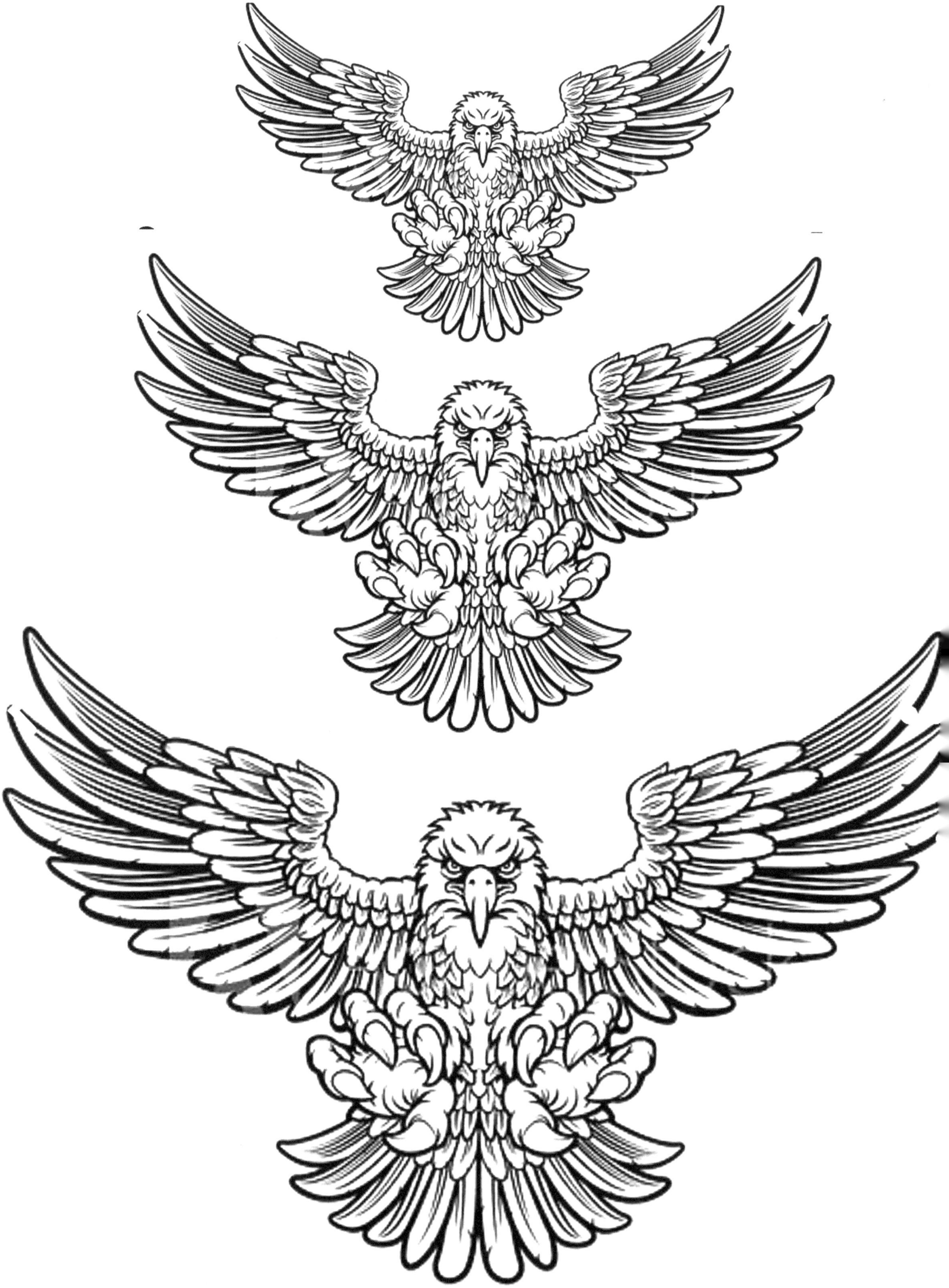

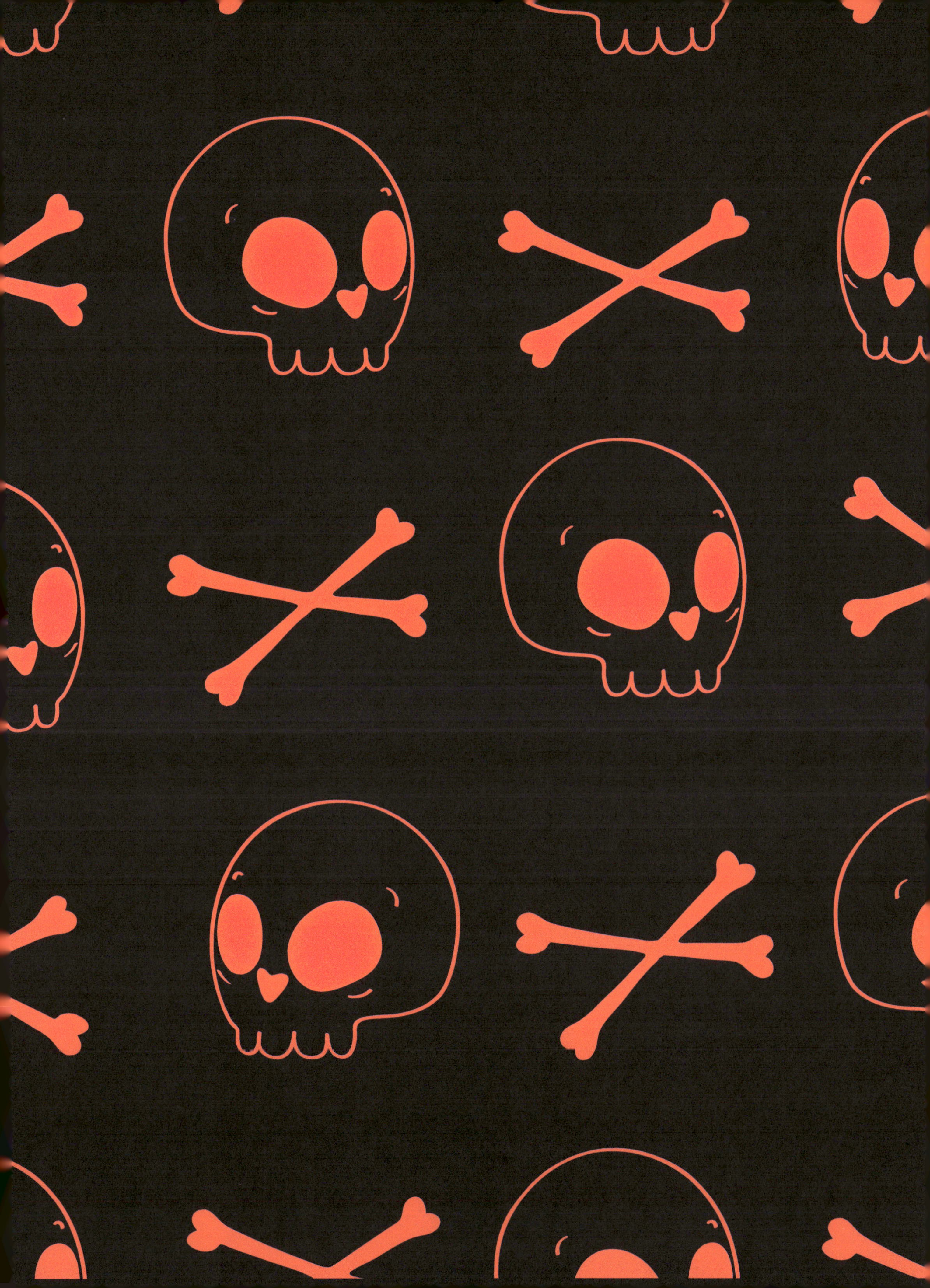

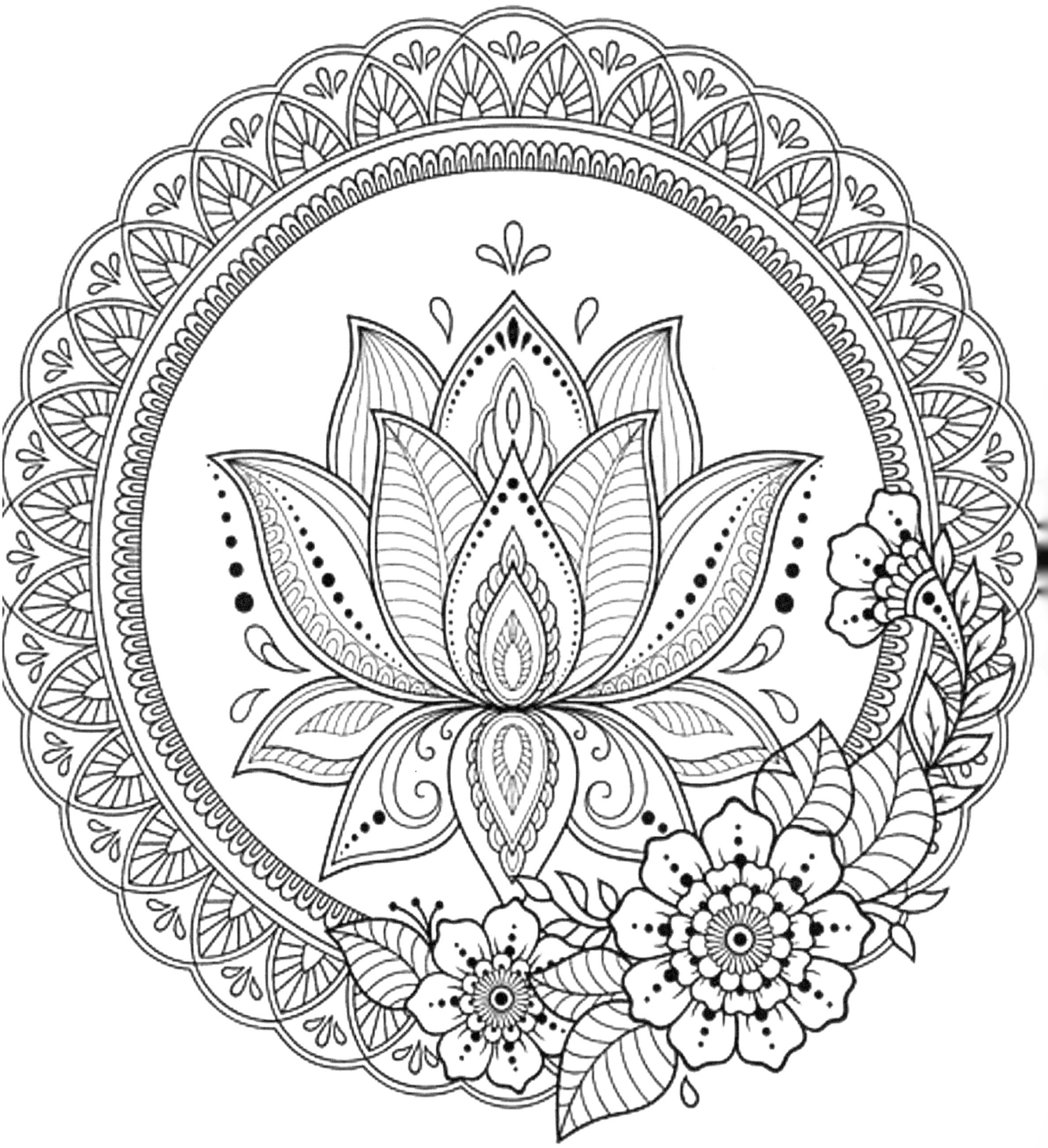

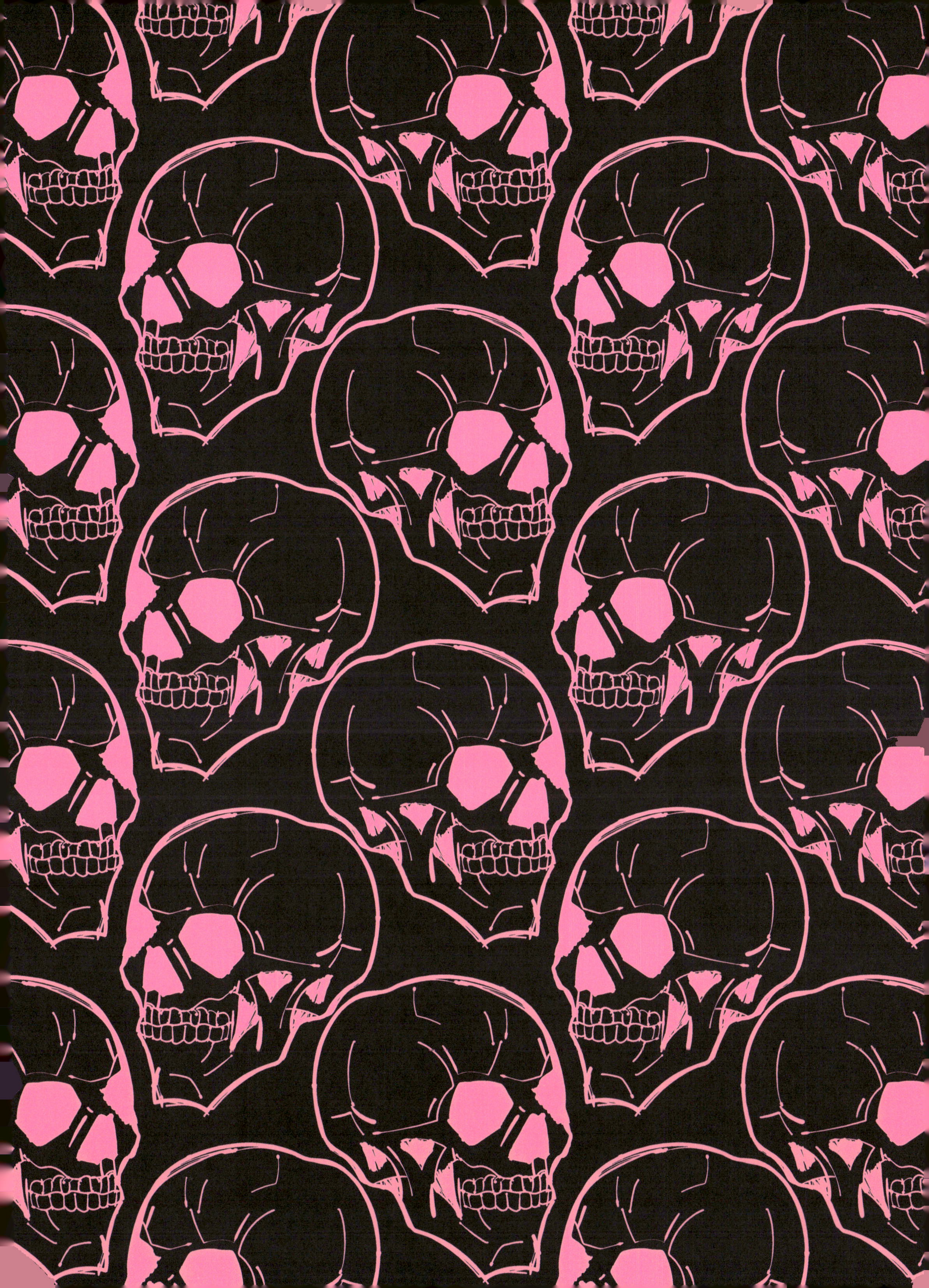

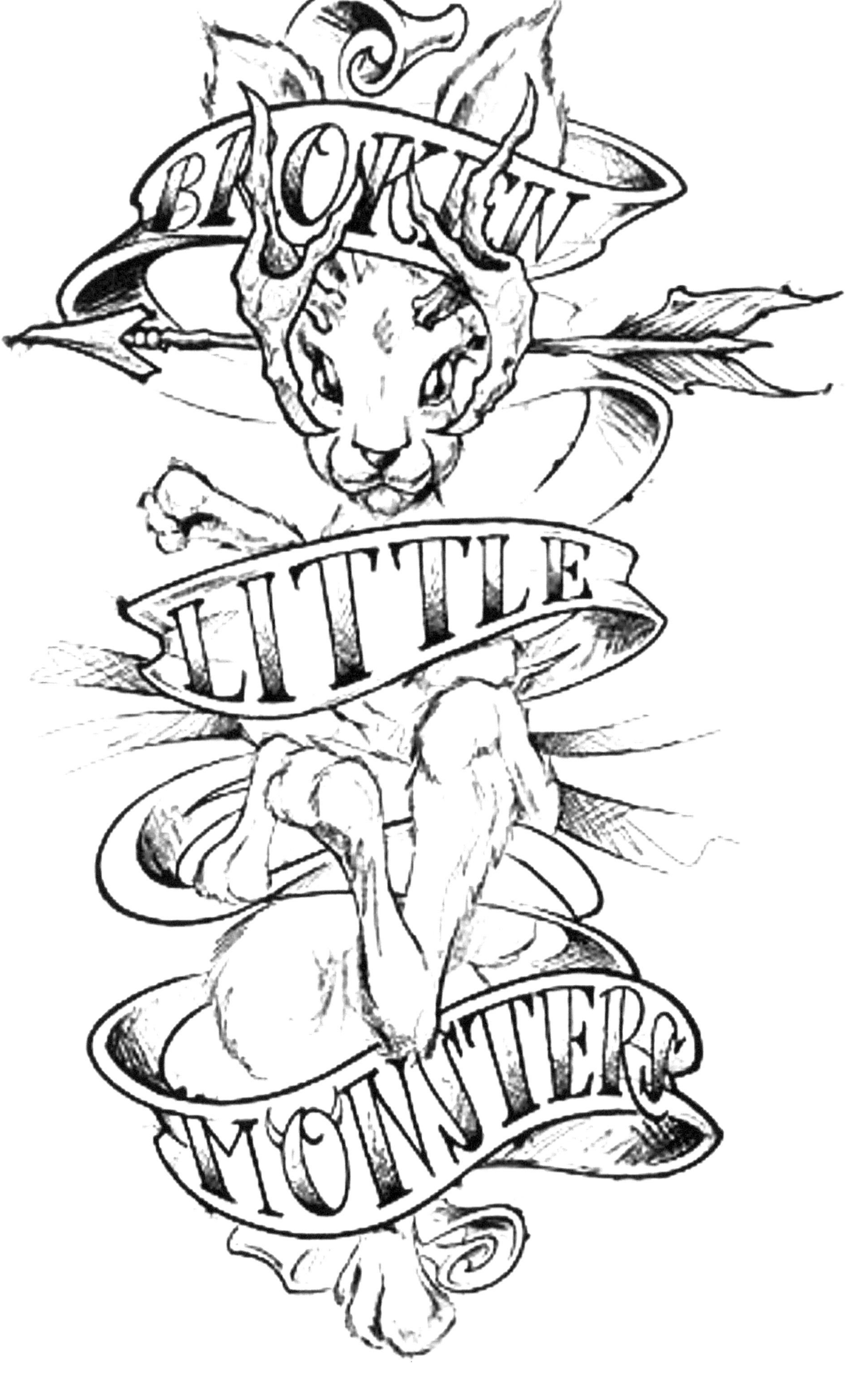
BROKEN
LITTLE
MONSTERS

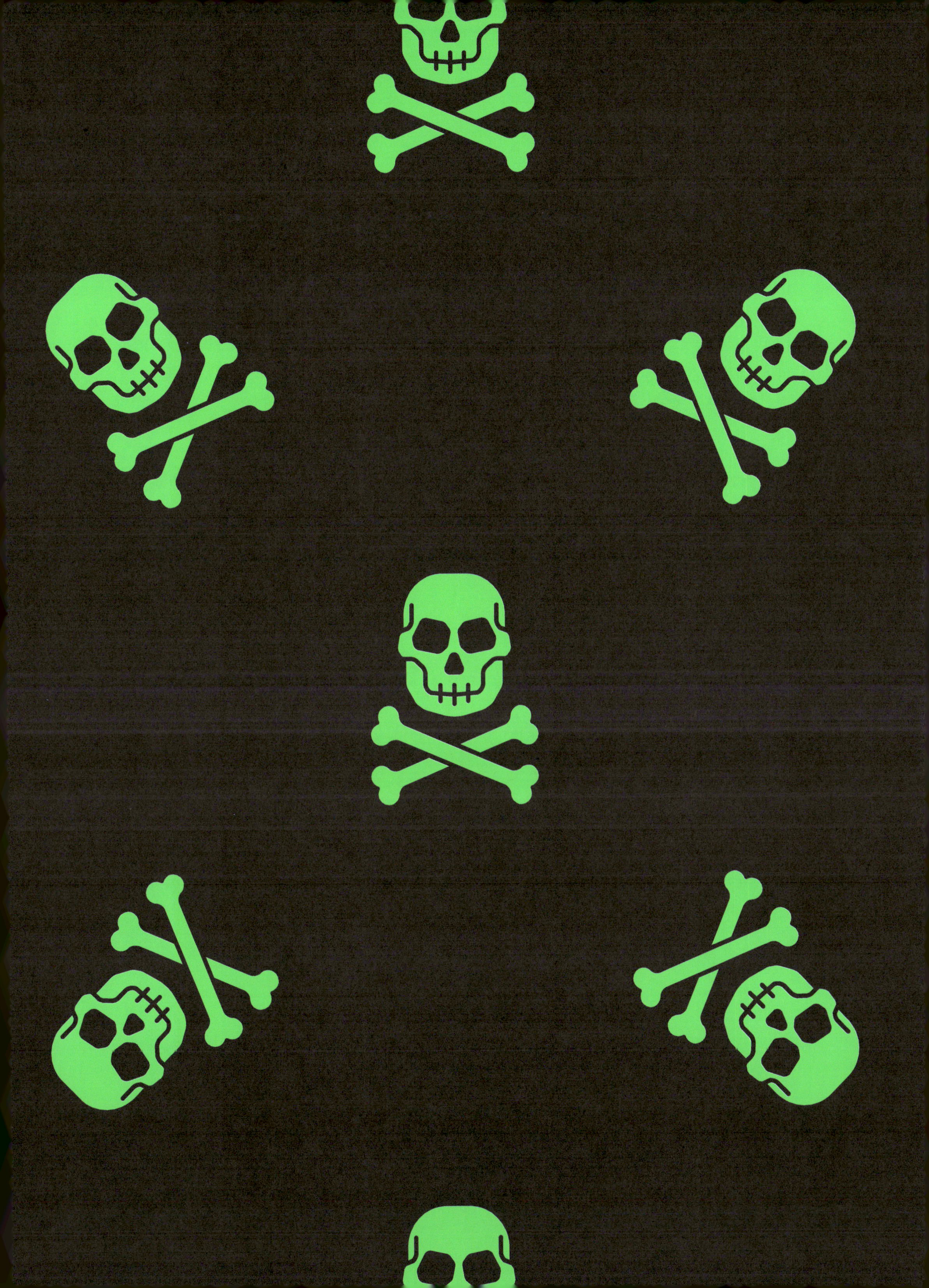

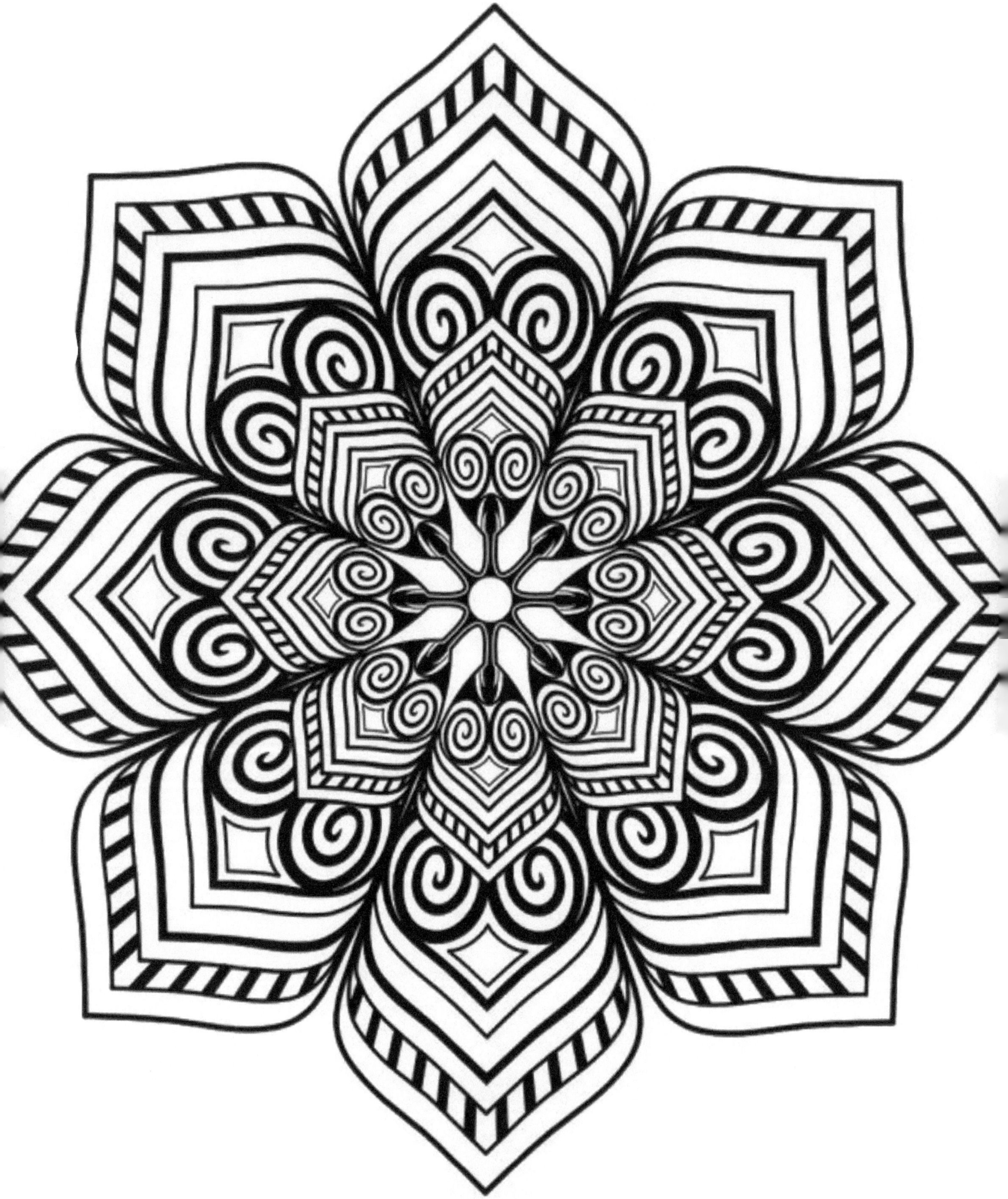

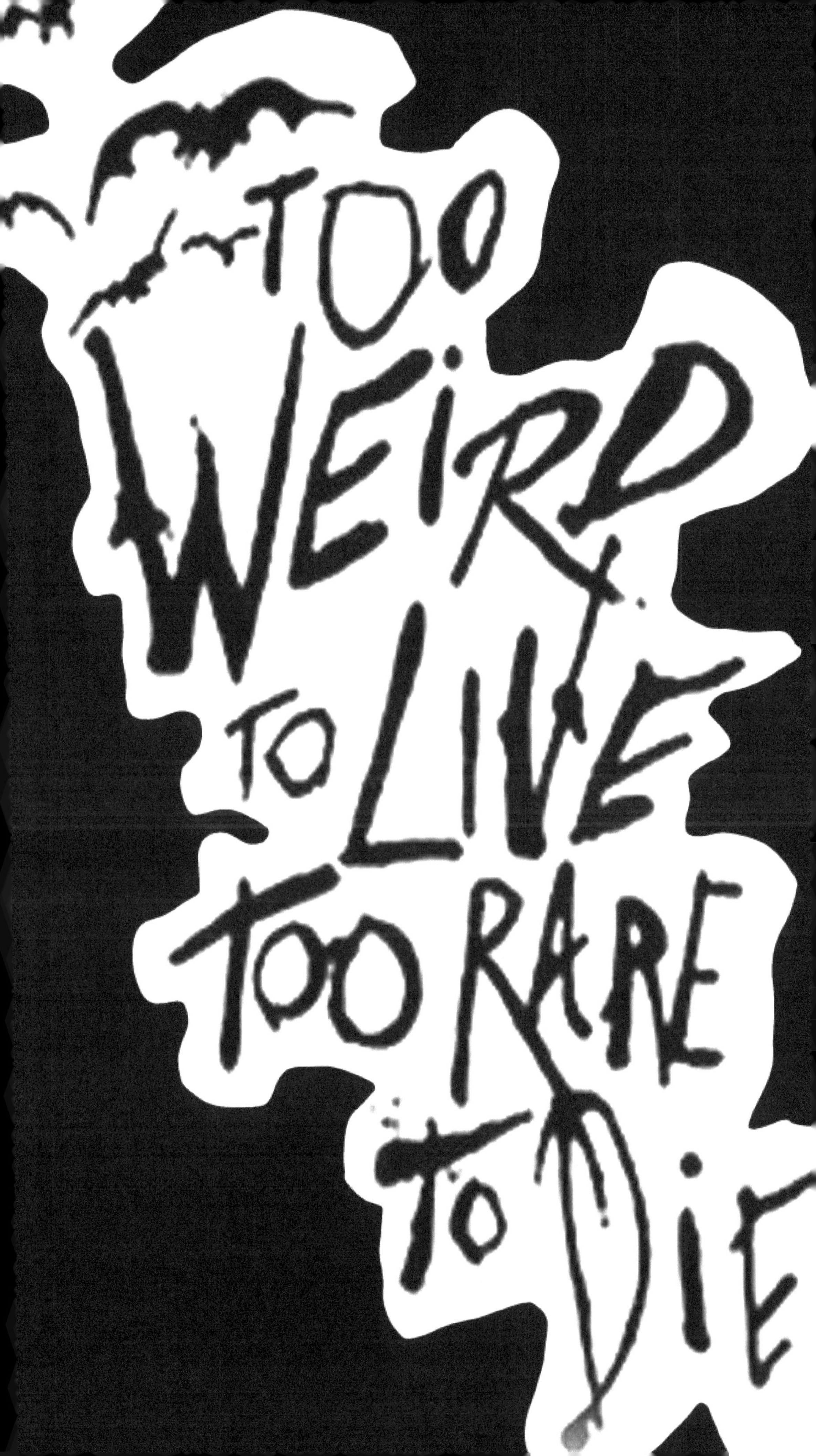
TOO
WEIRD
TO LIVE
TOO RARE
TO DIE

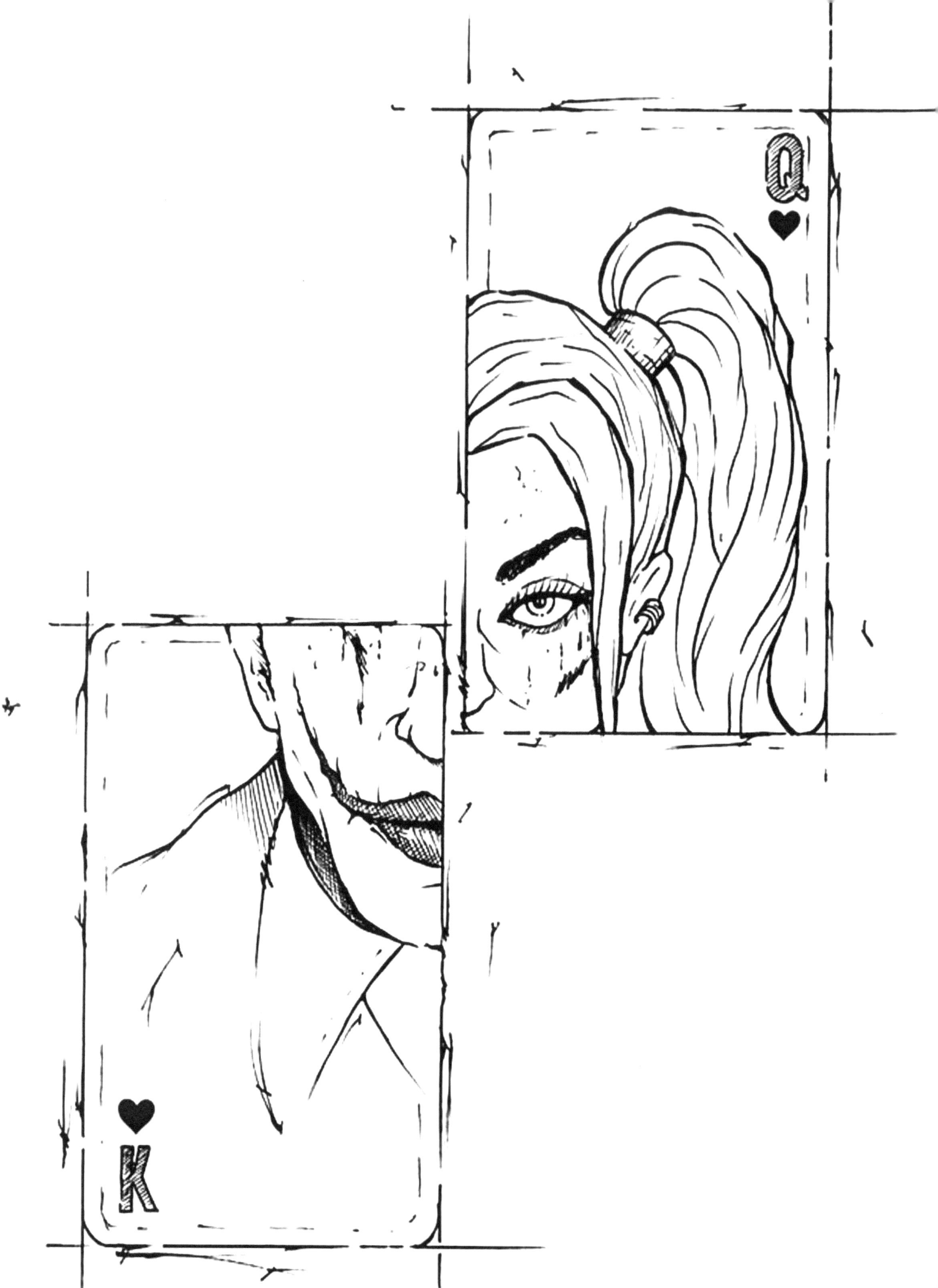
Q
K

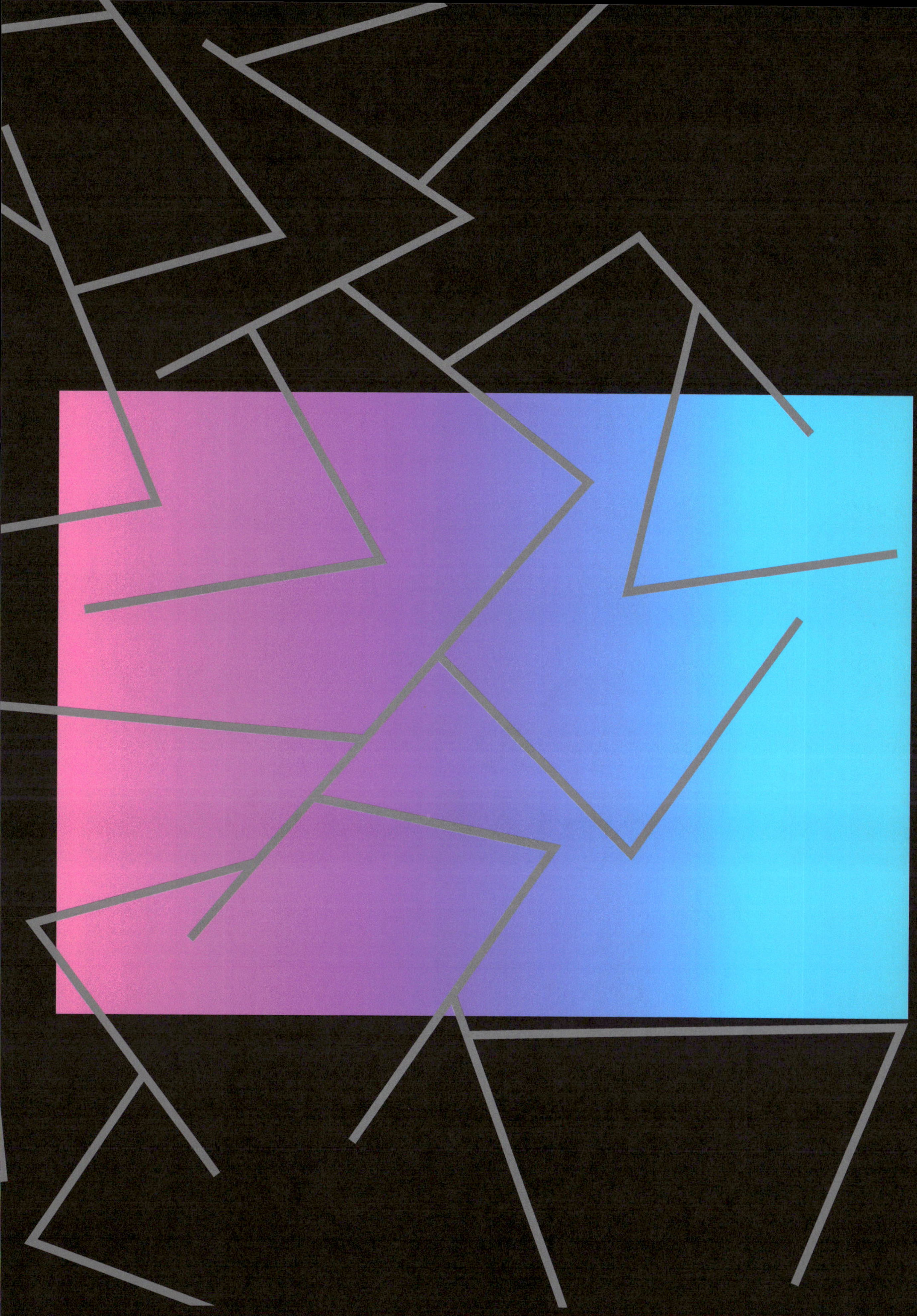

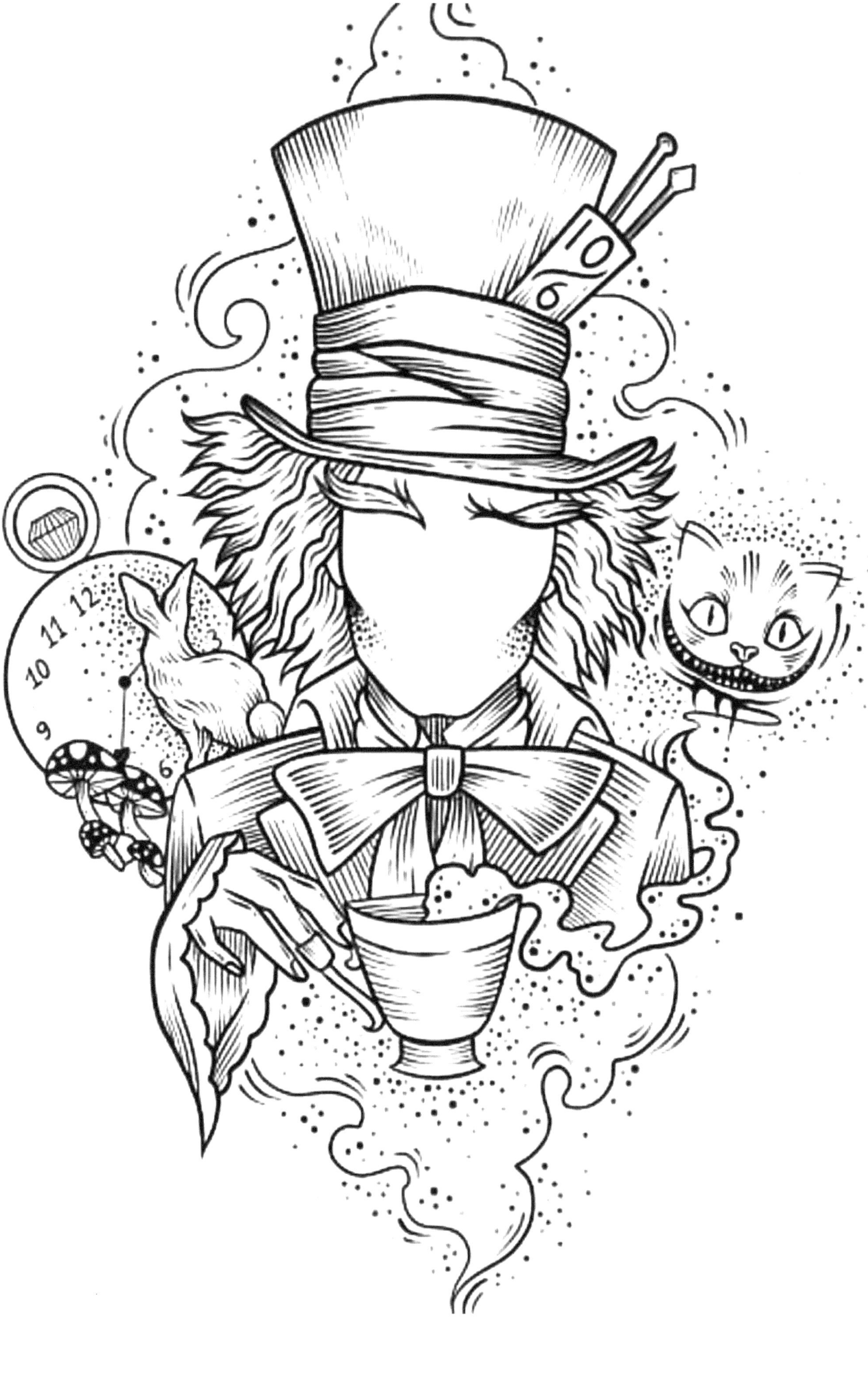
12
11
10
9
6
10/6

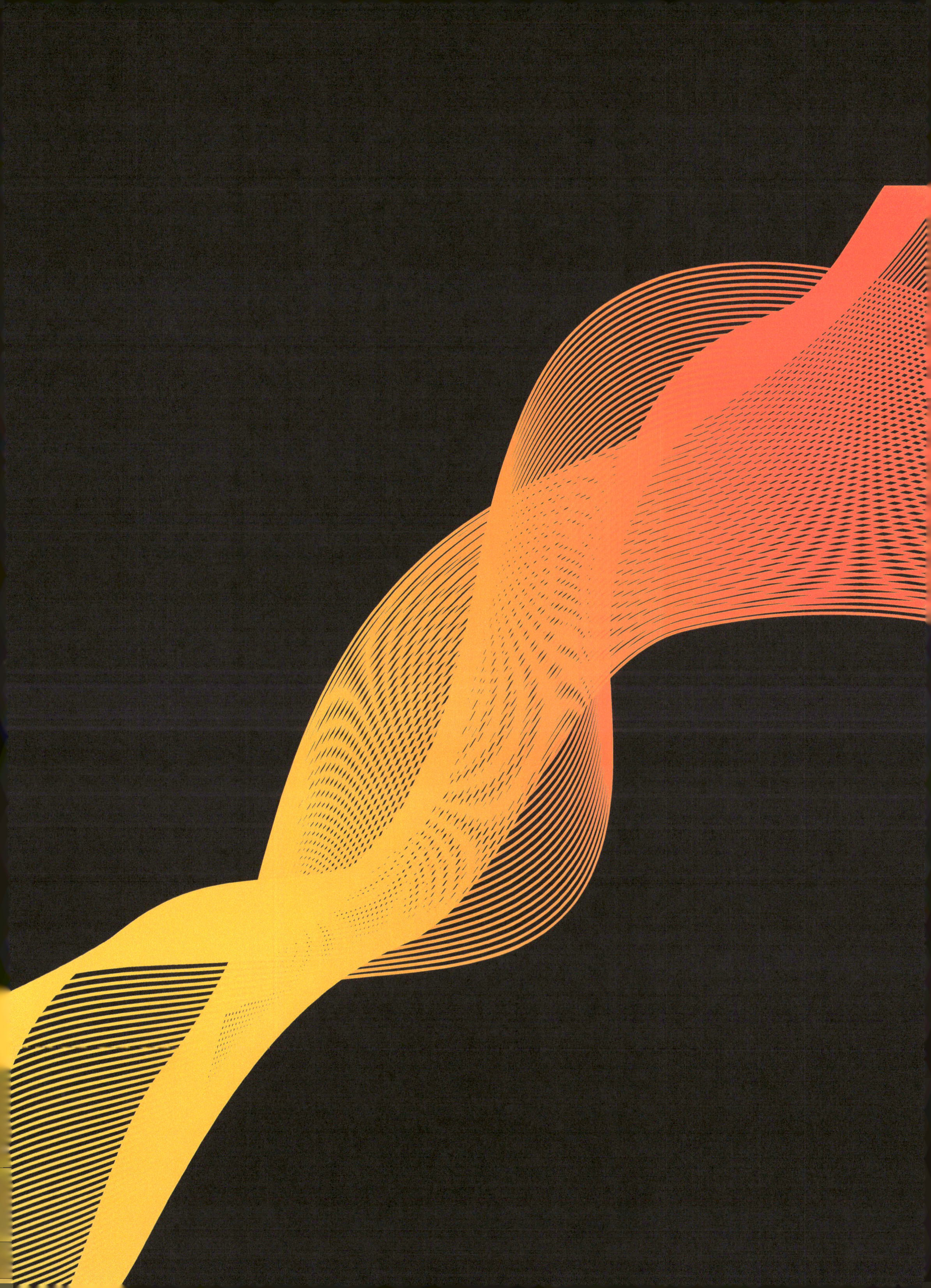

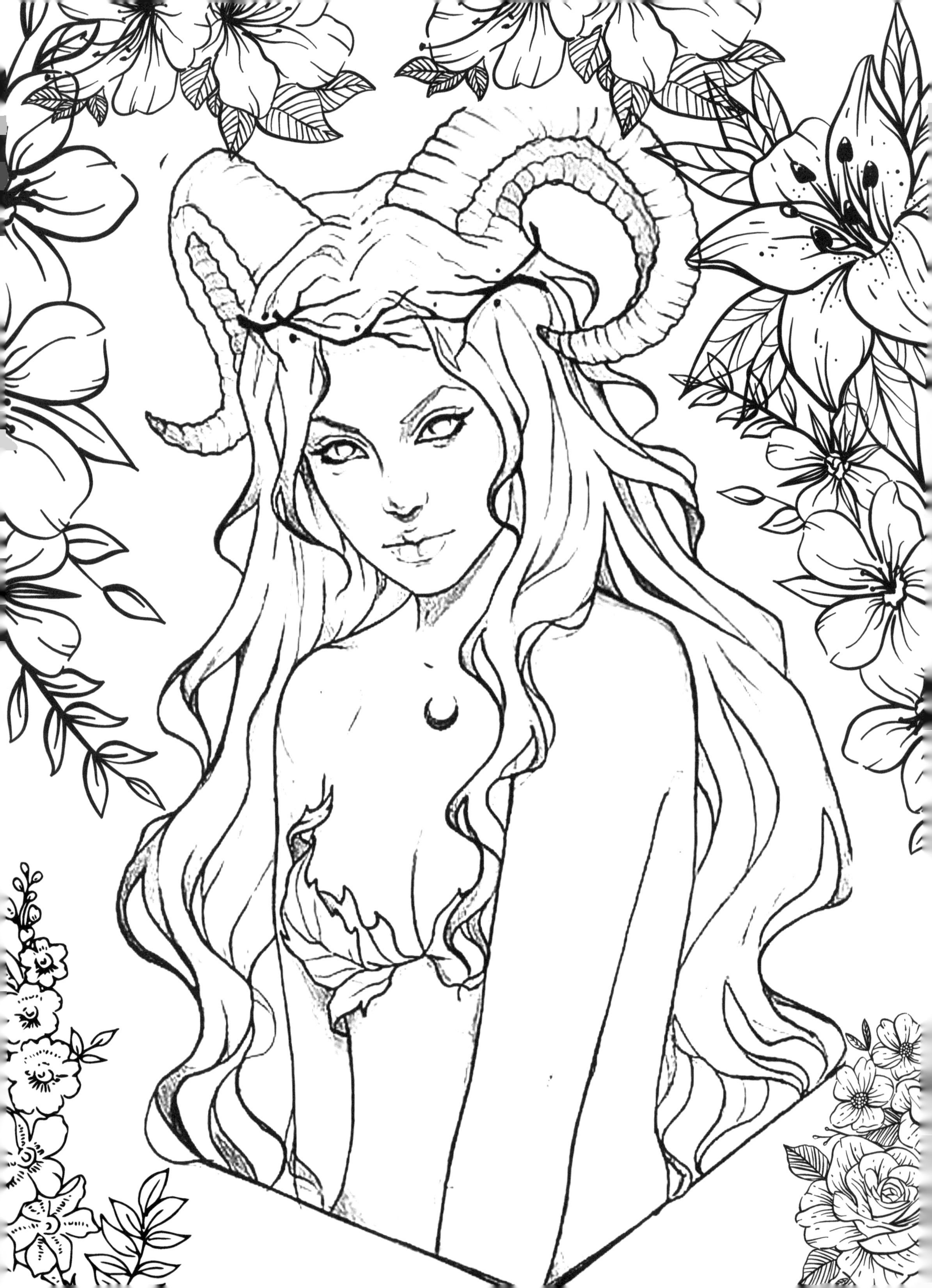

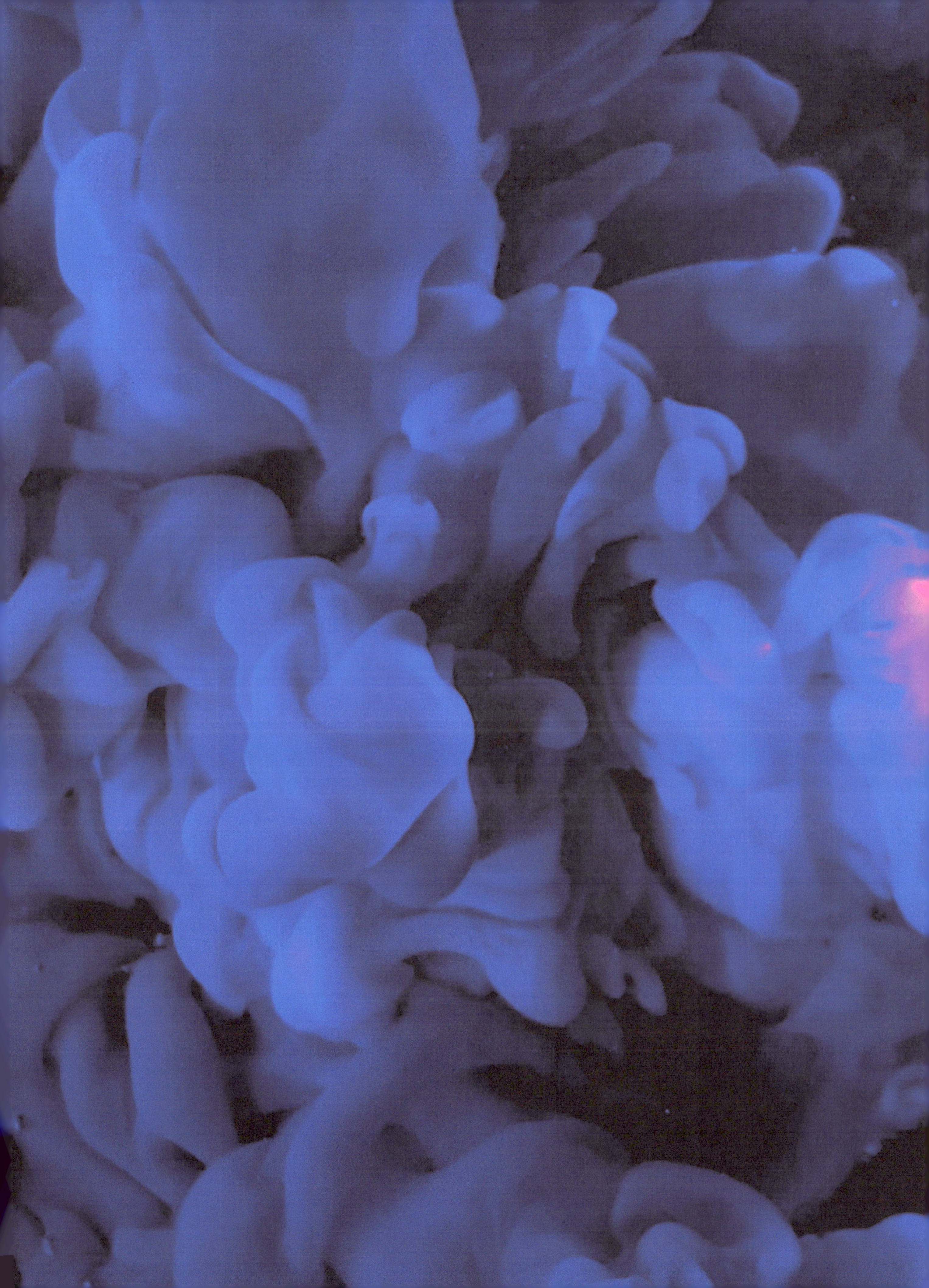

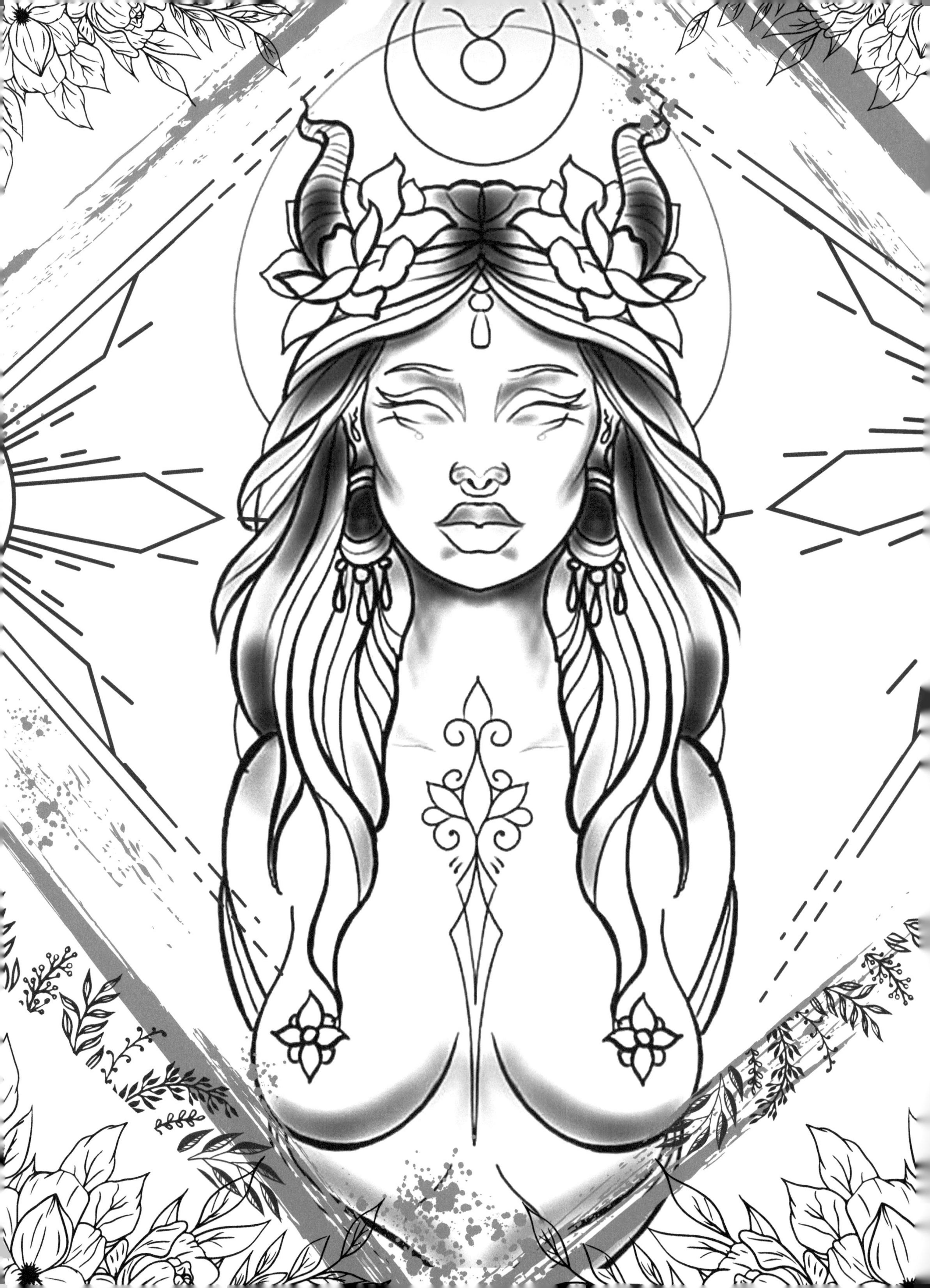

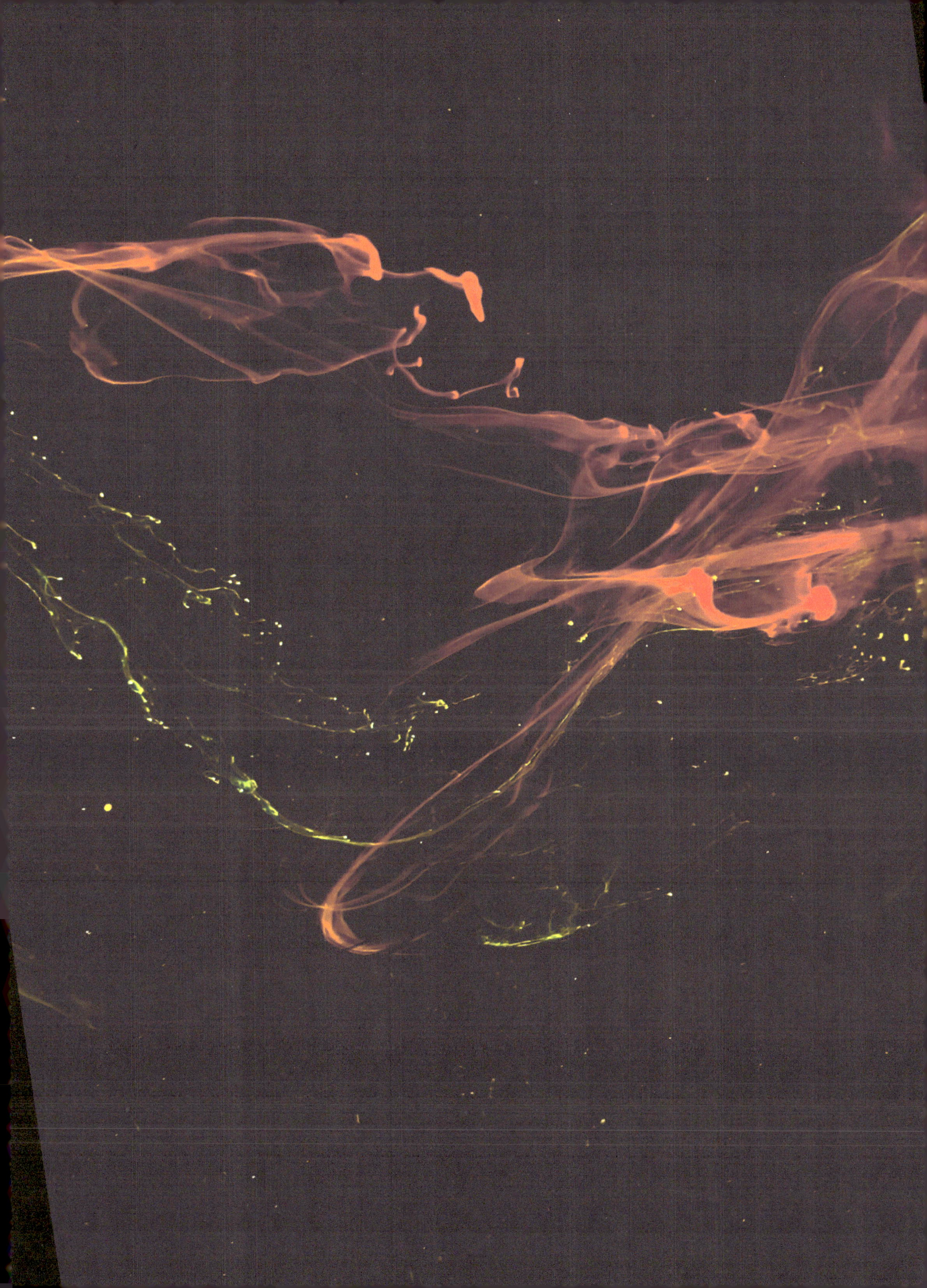

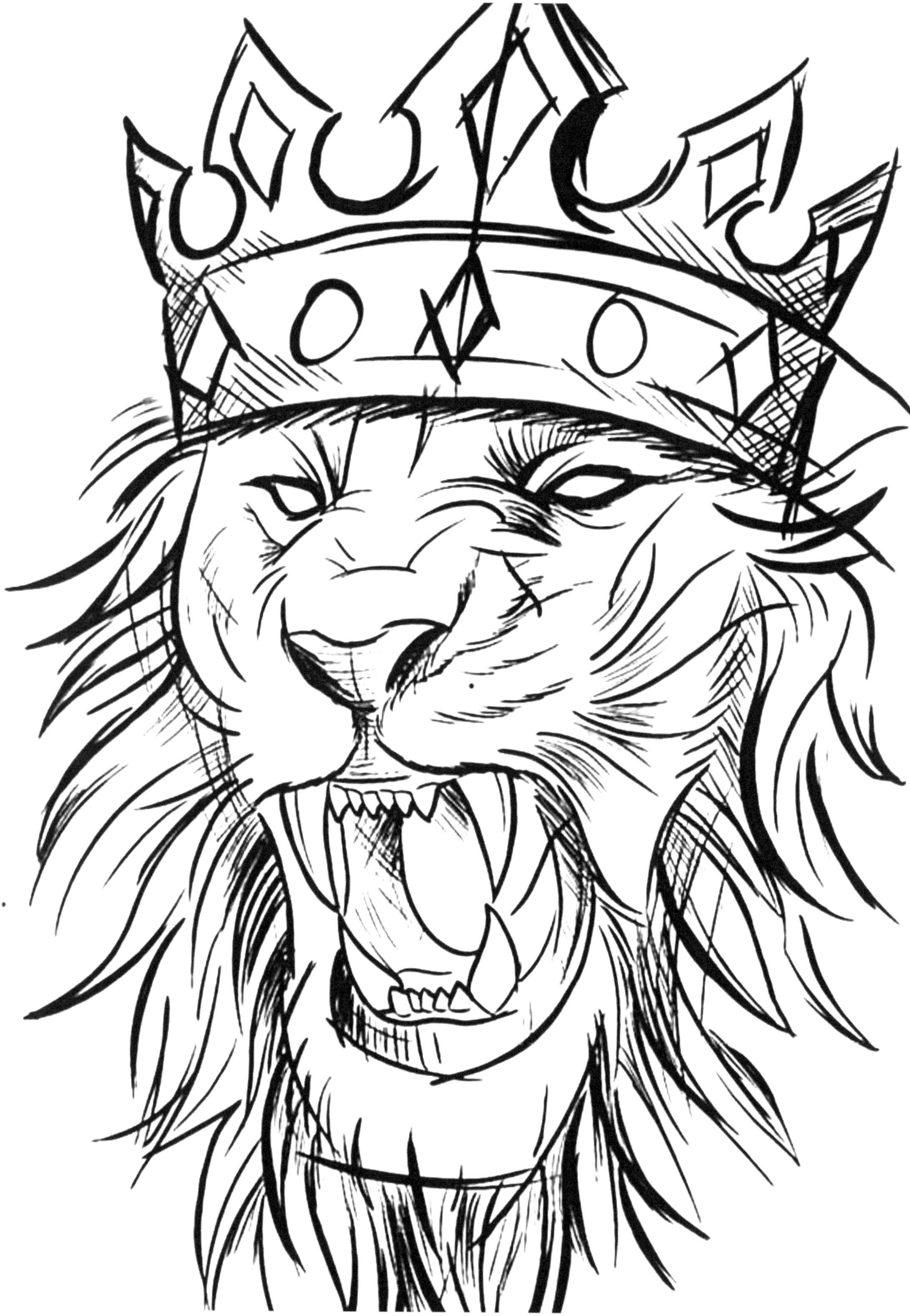

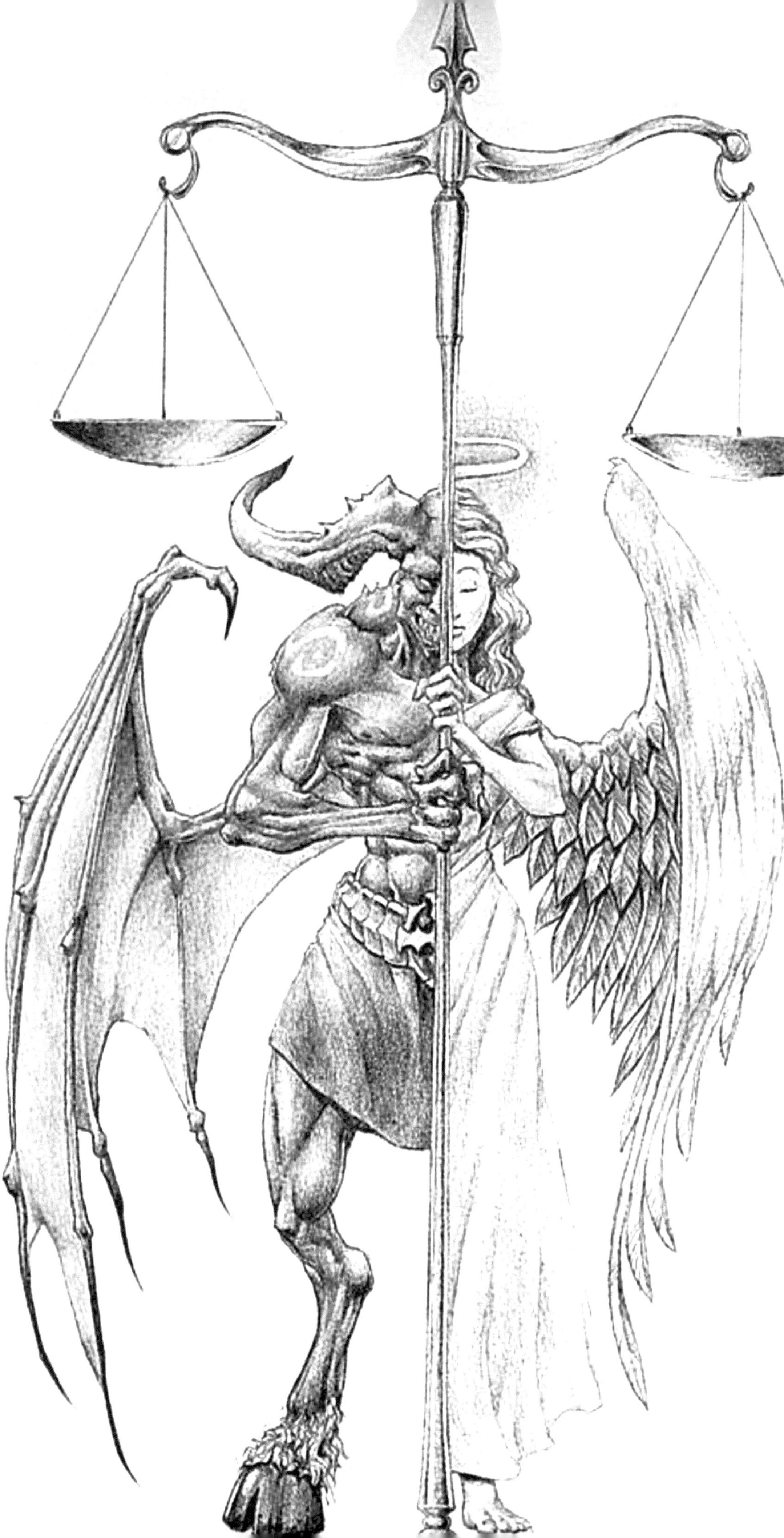

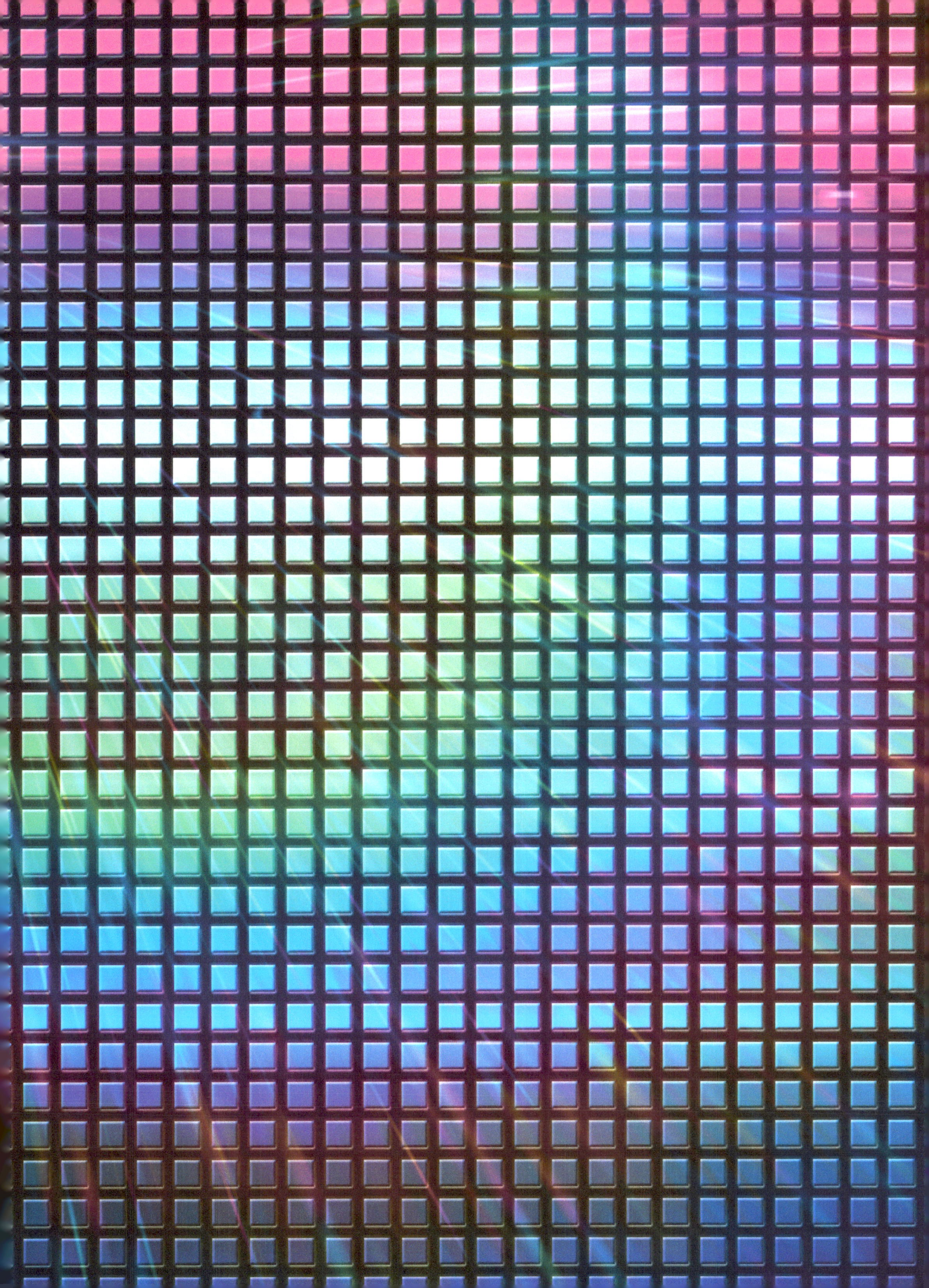

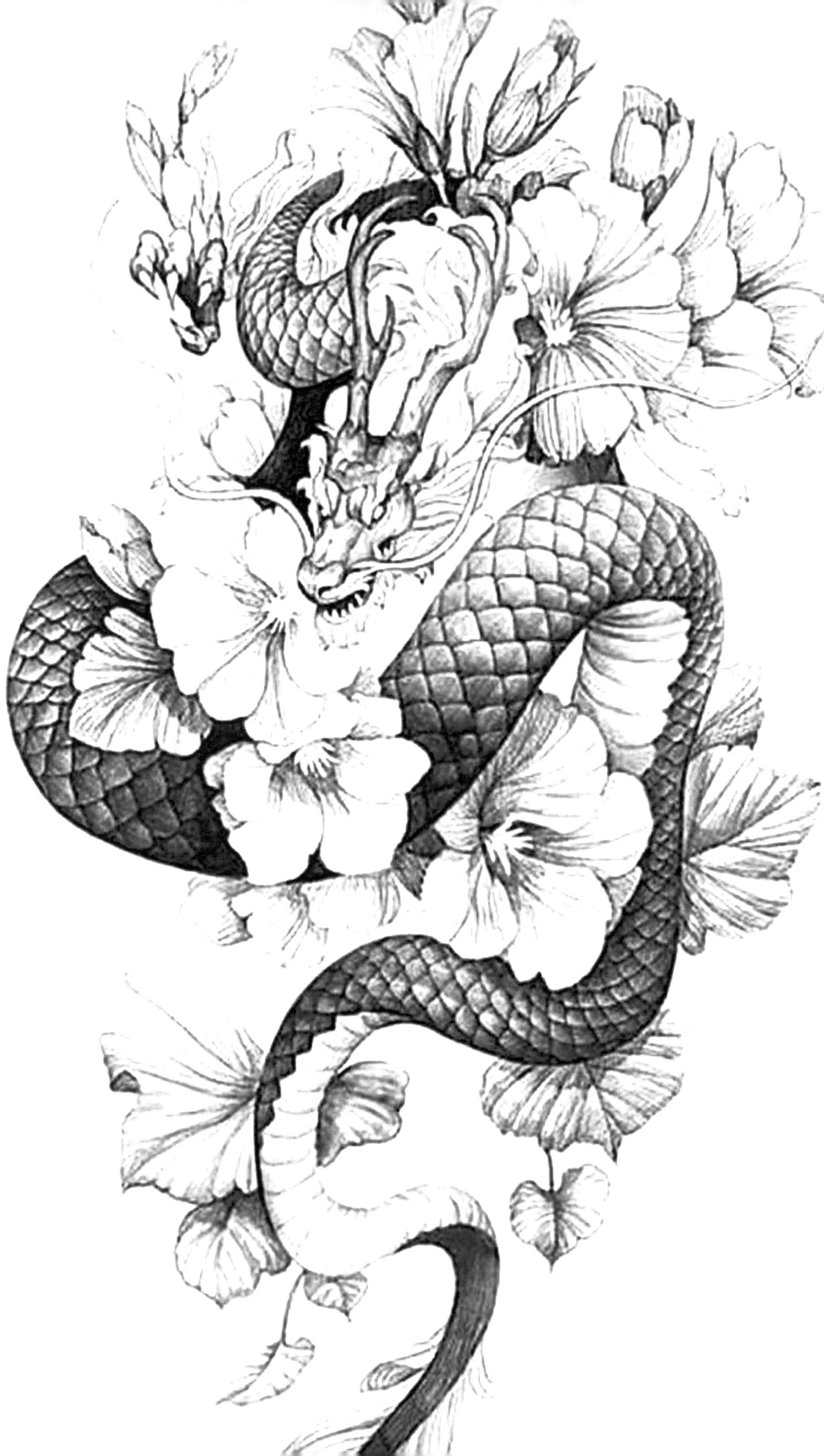

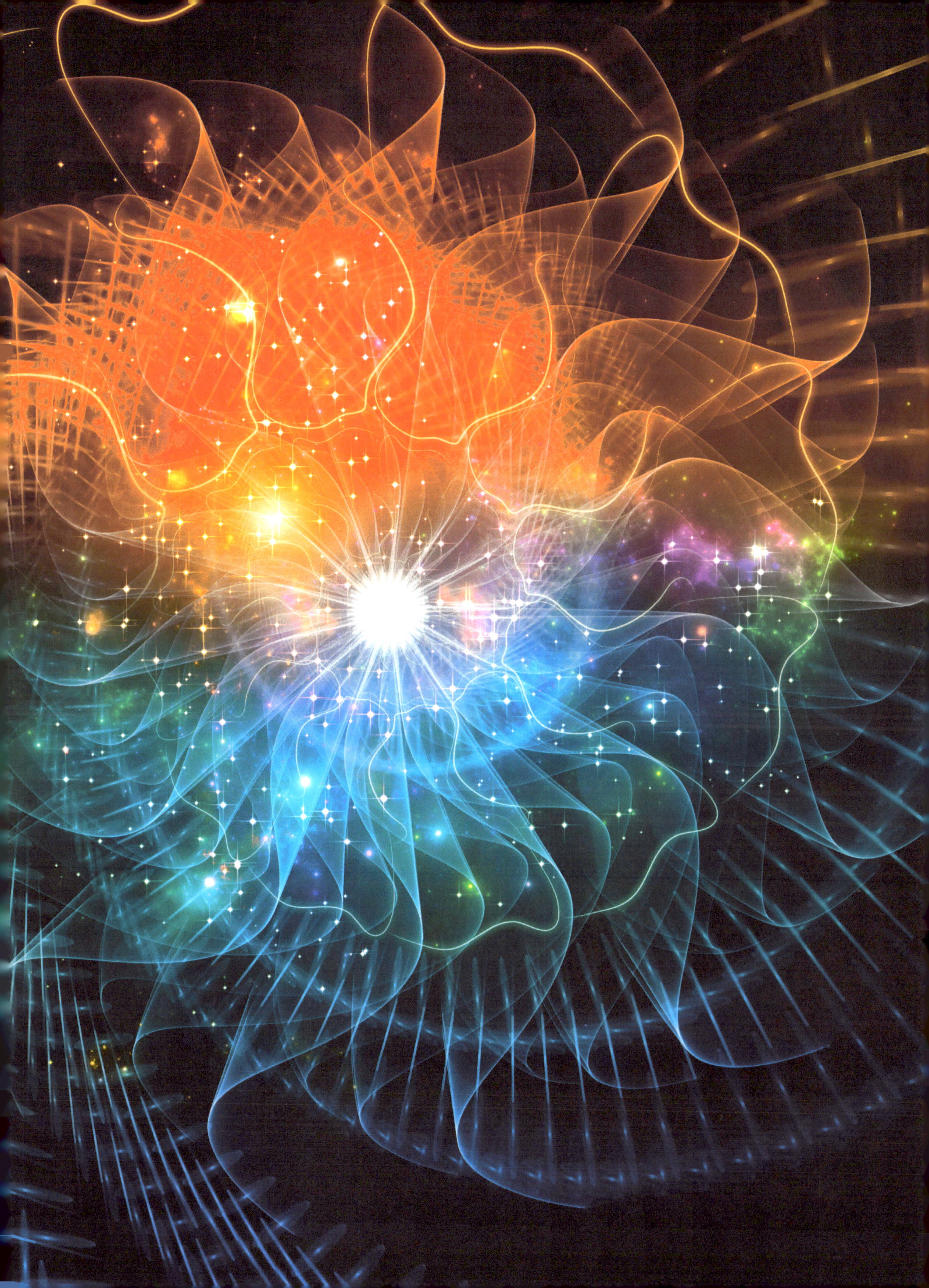

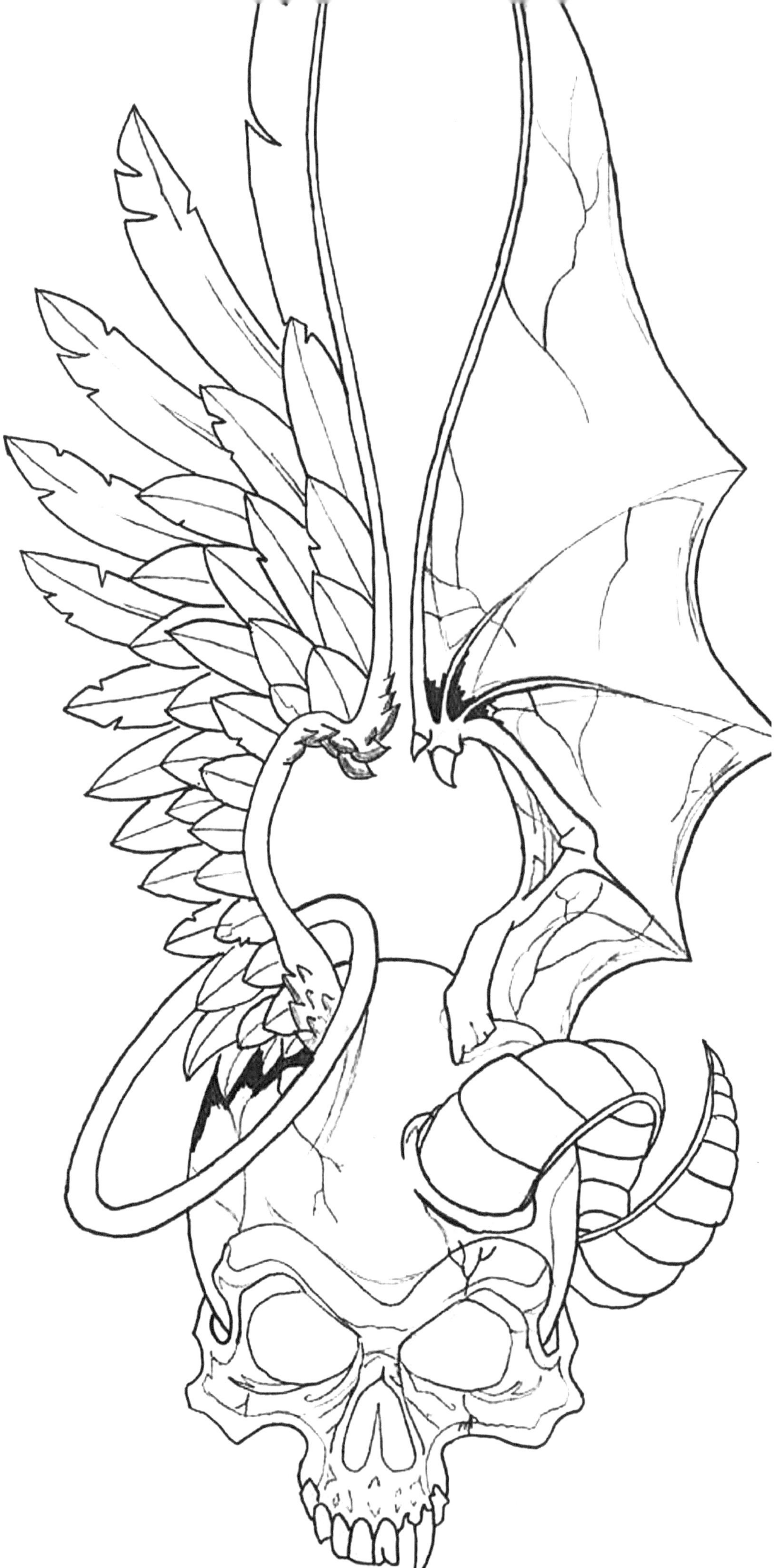

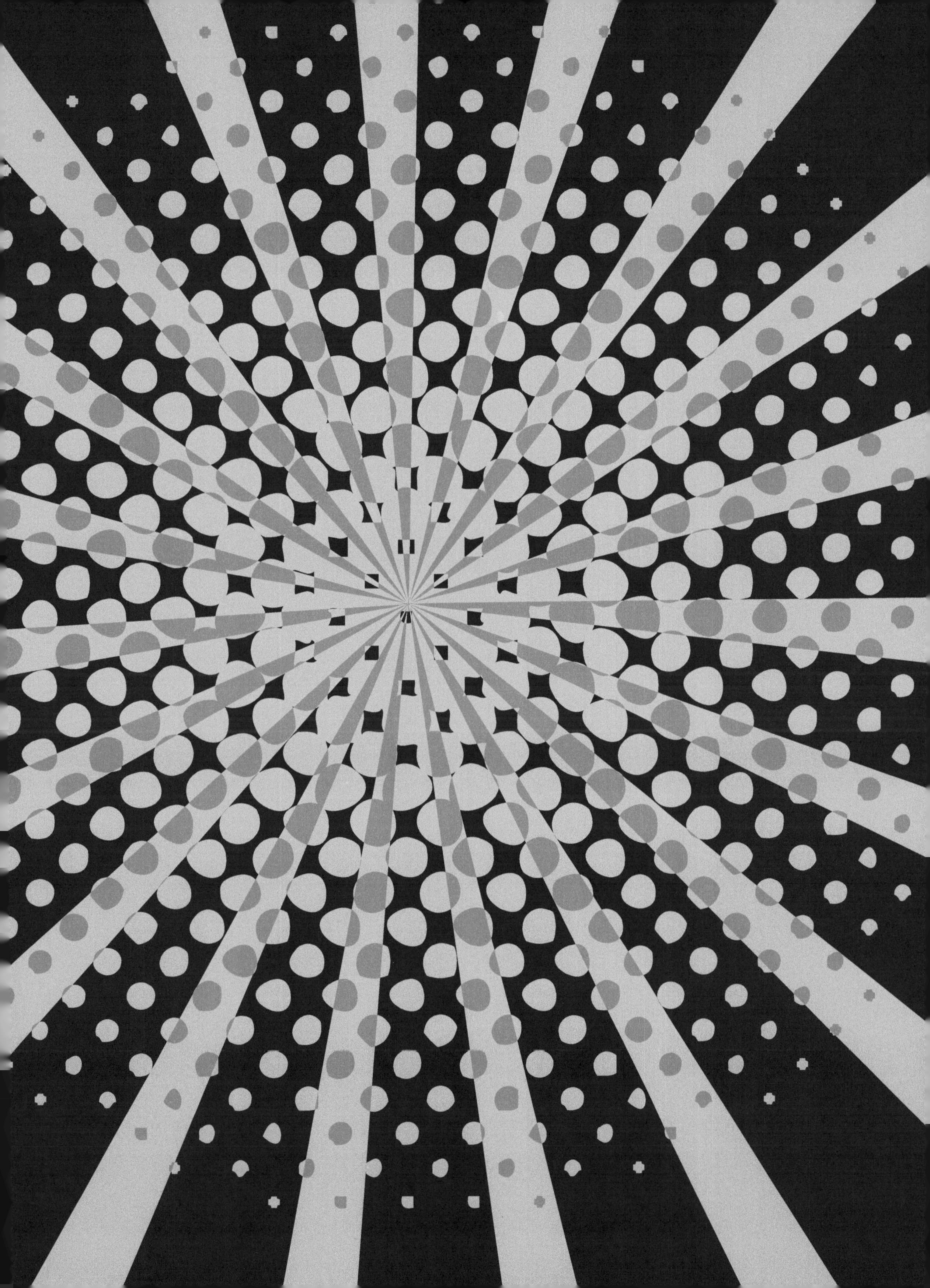

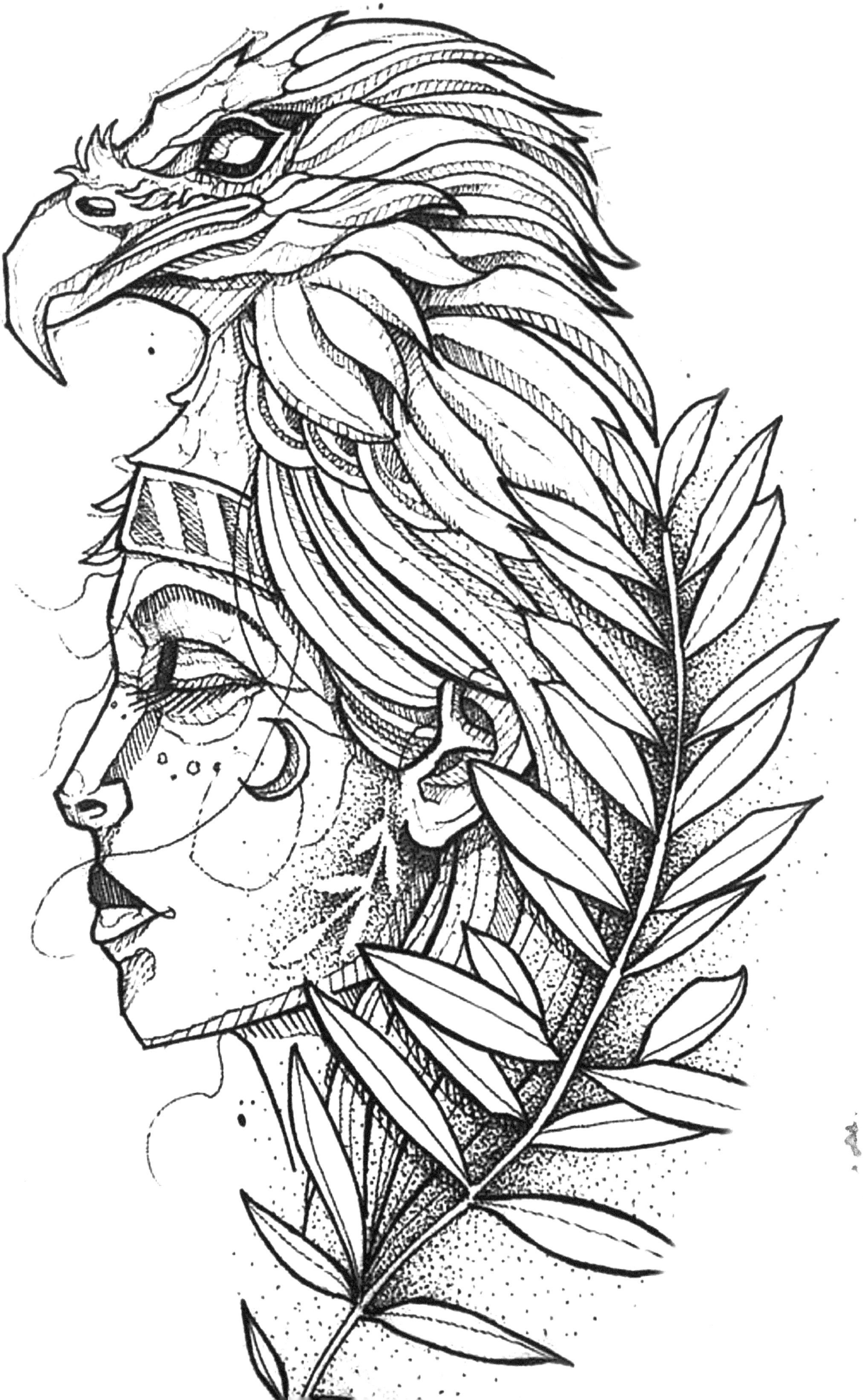

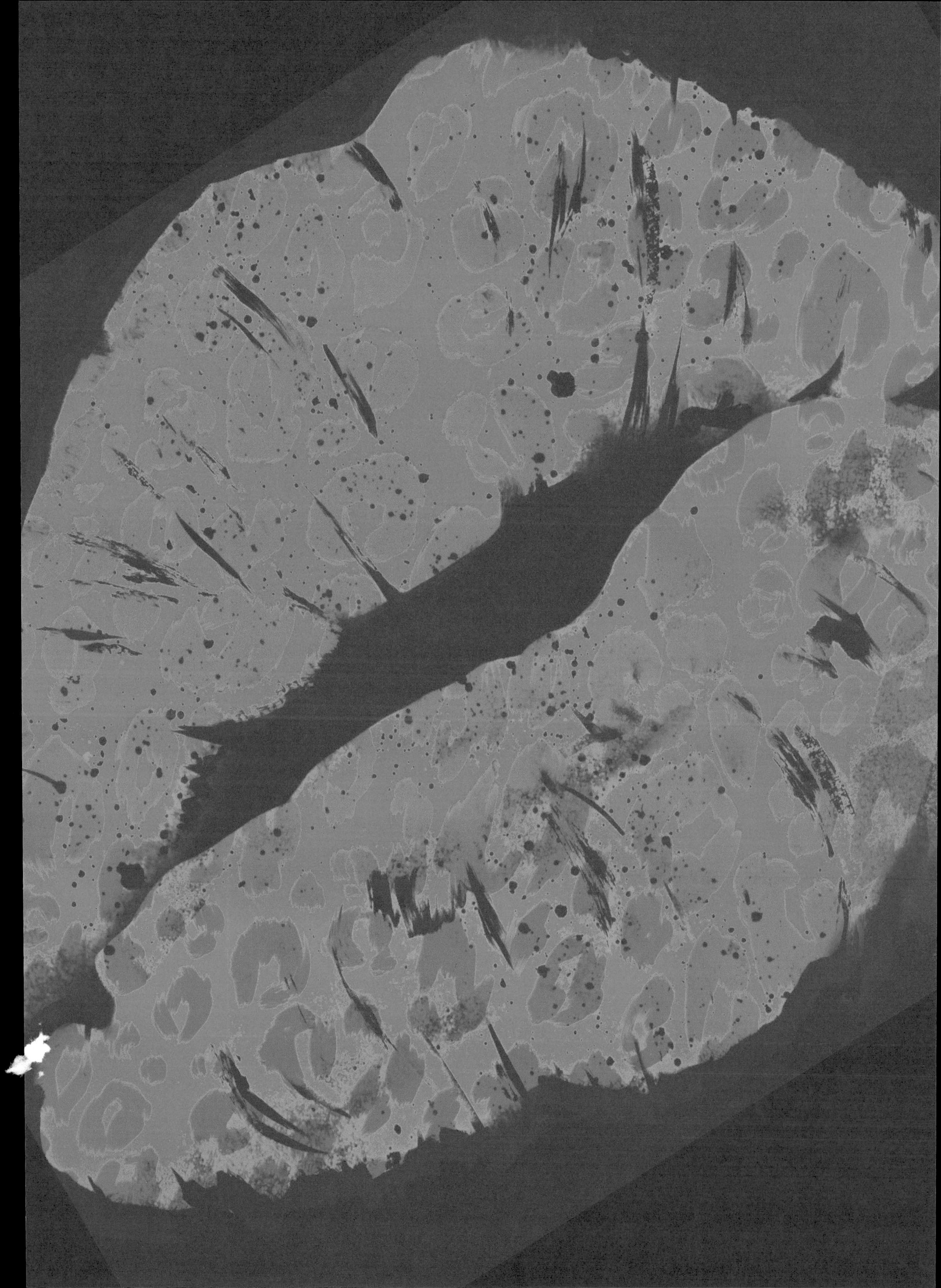

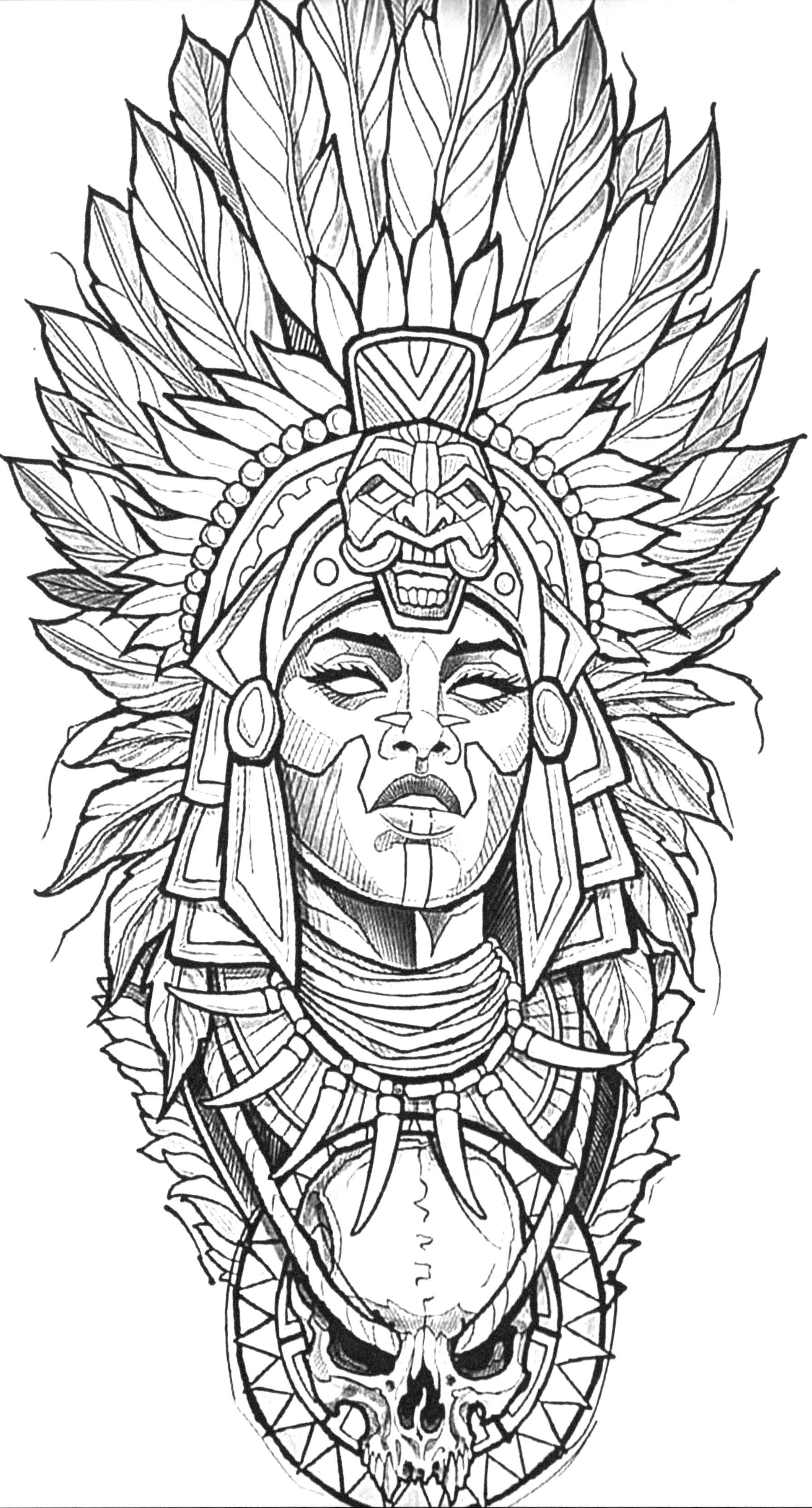

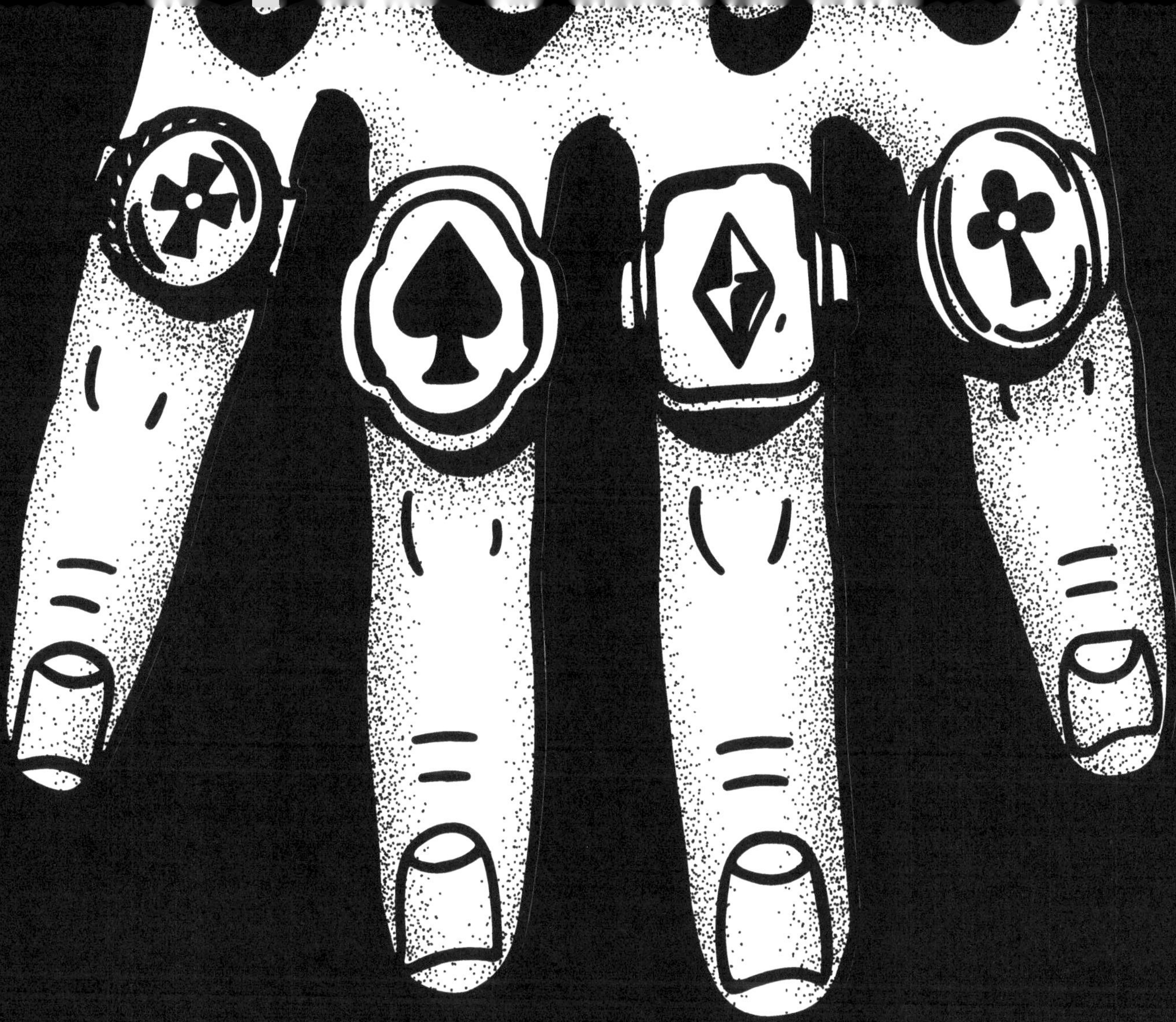

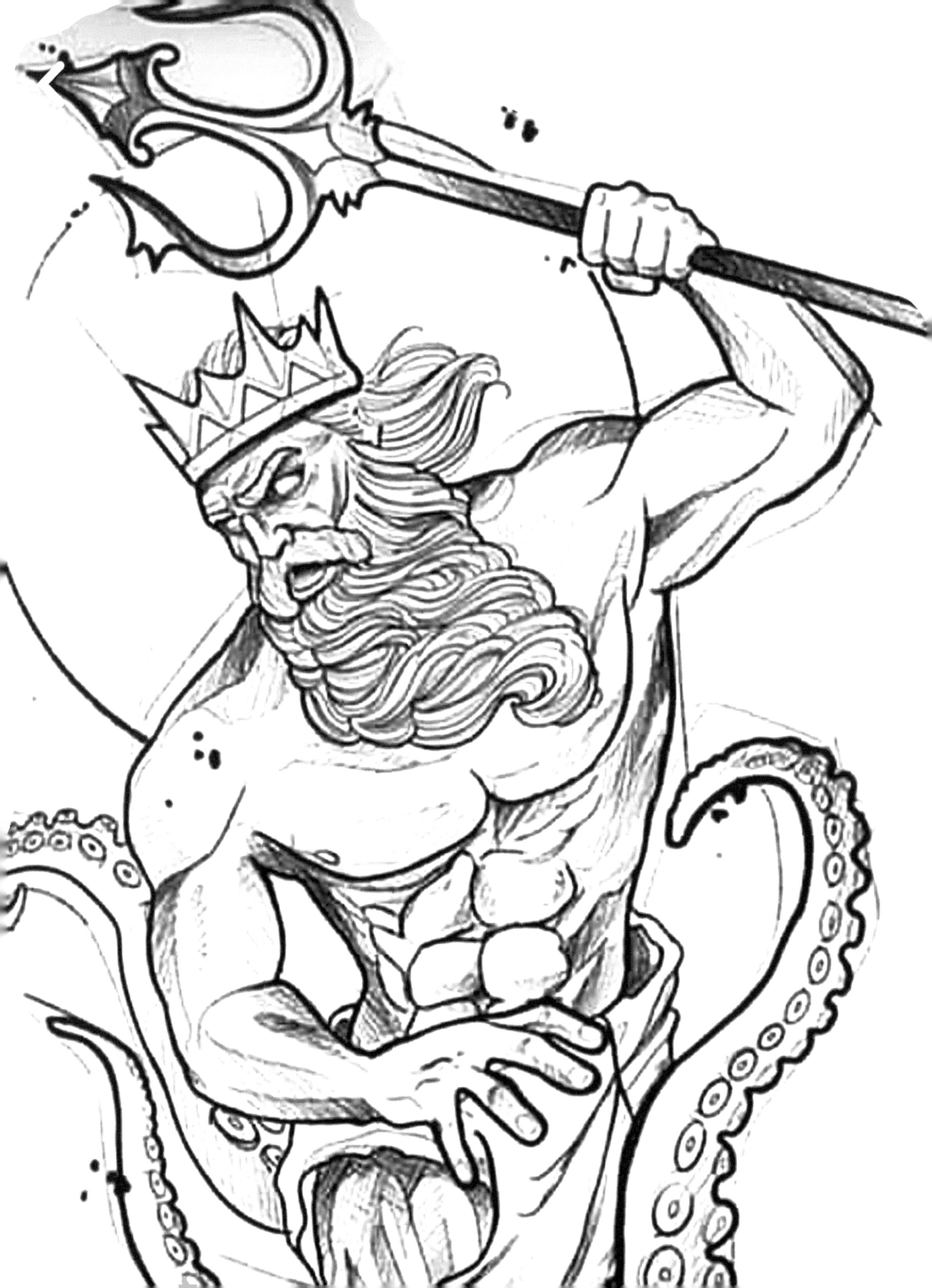

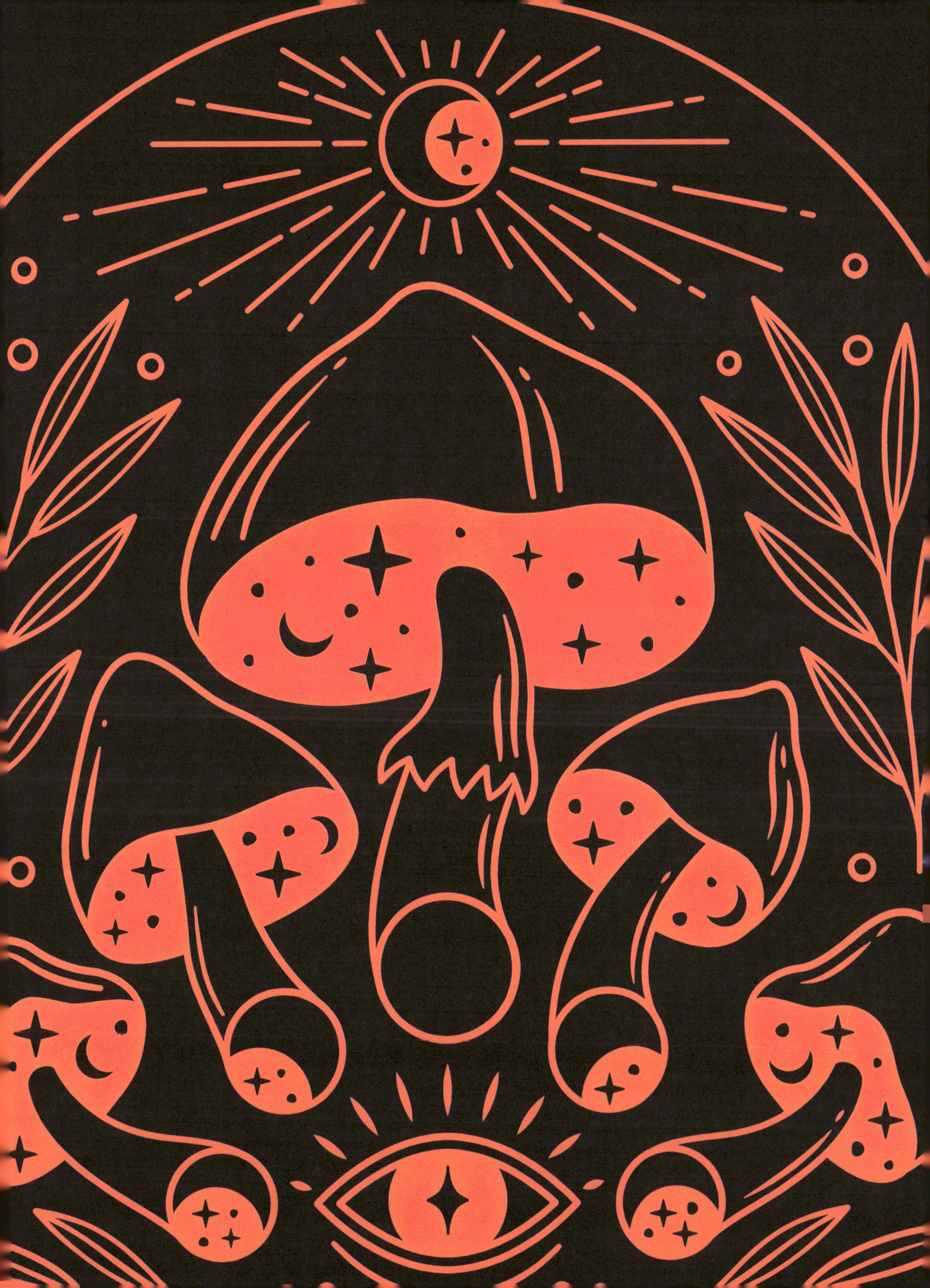

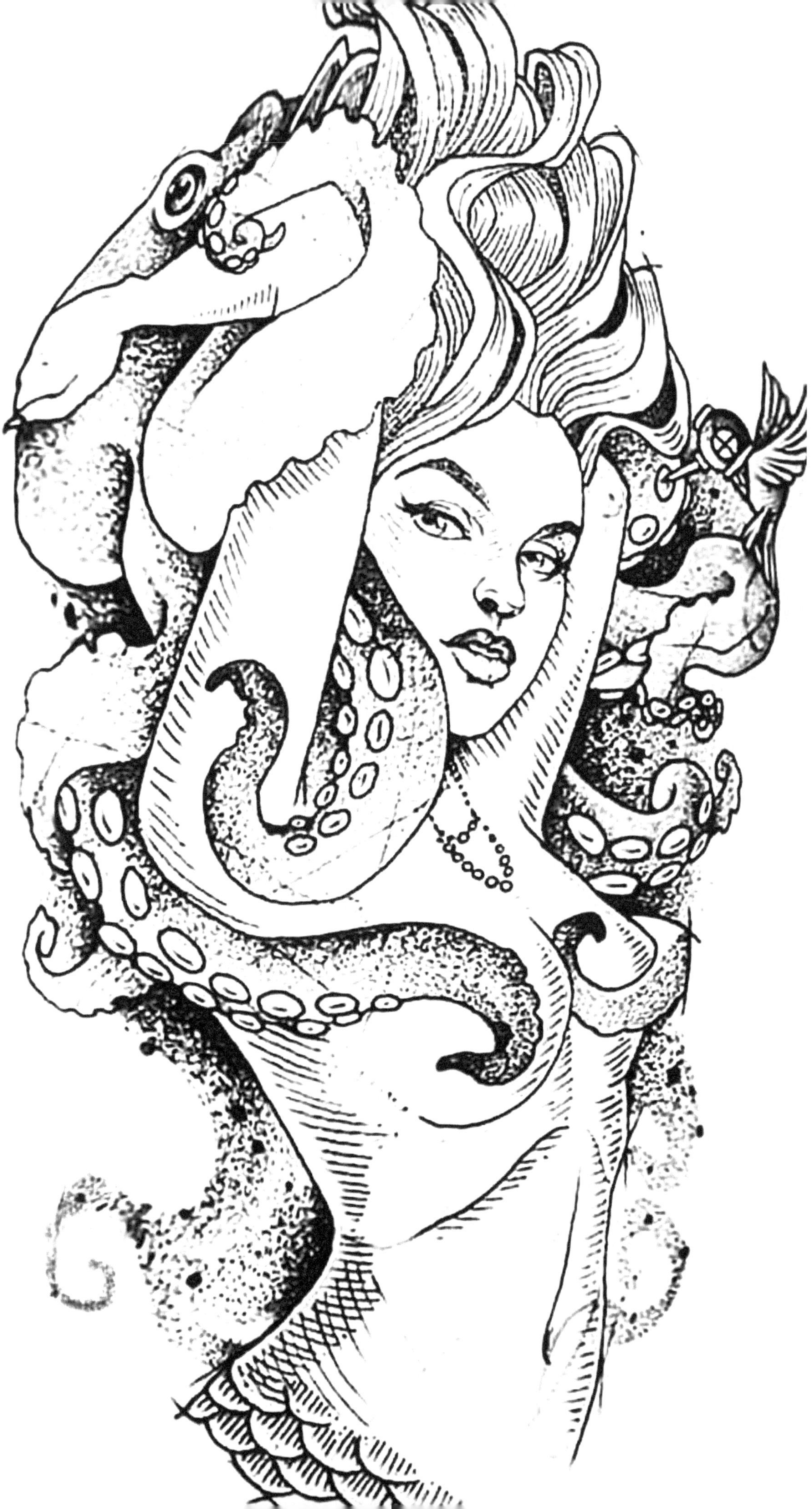

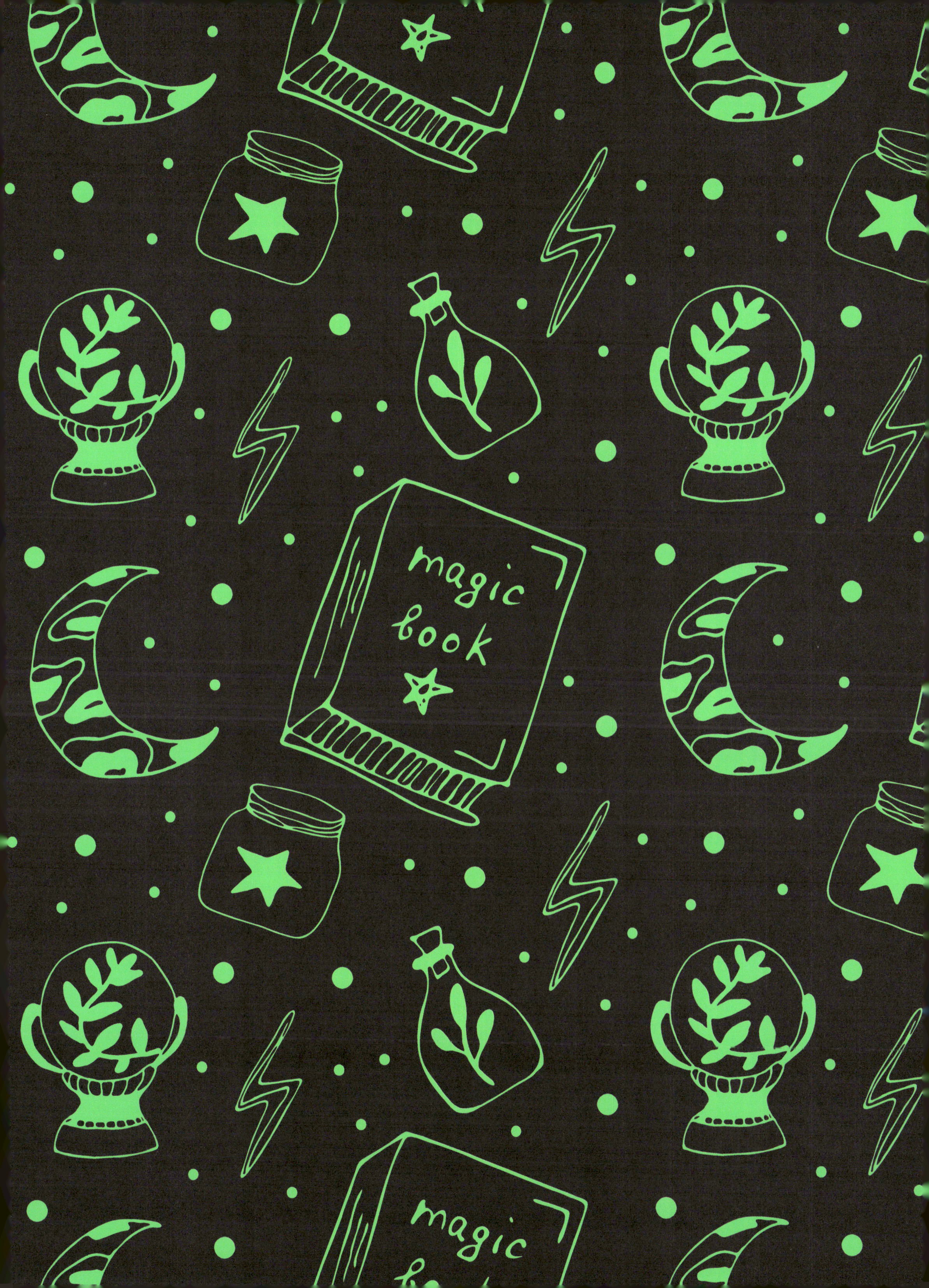
magic
book
magic

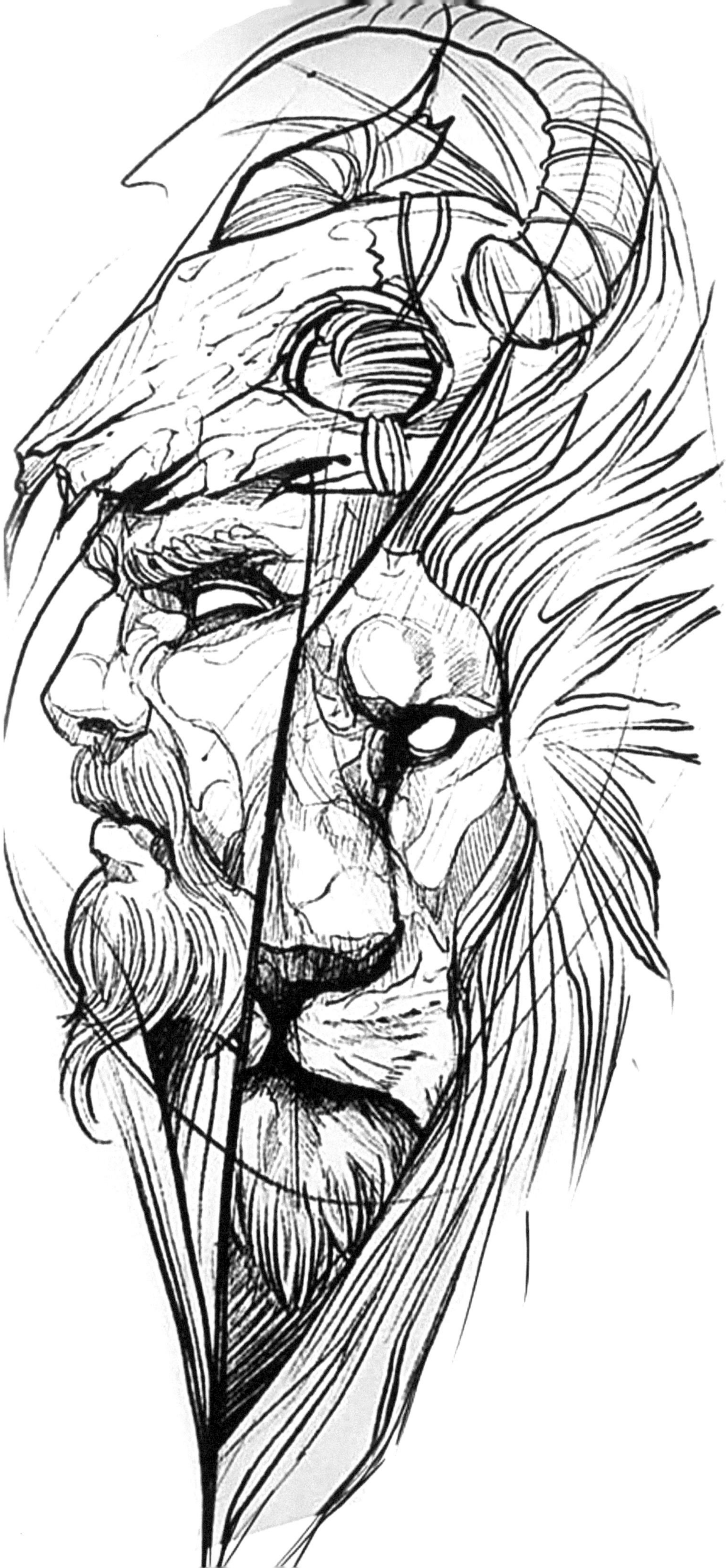

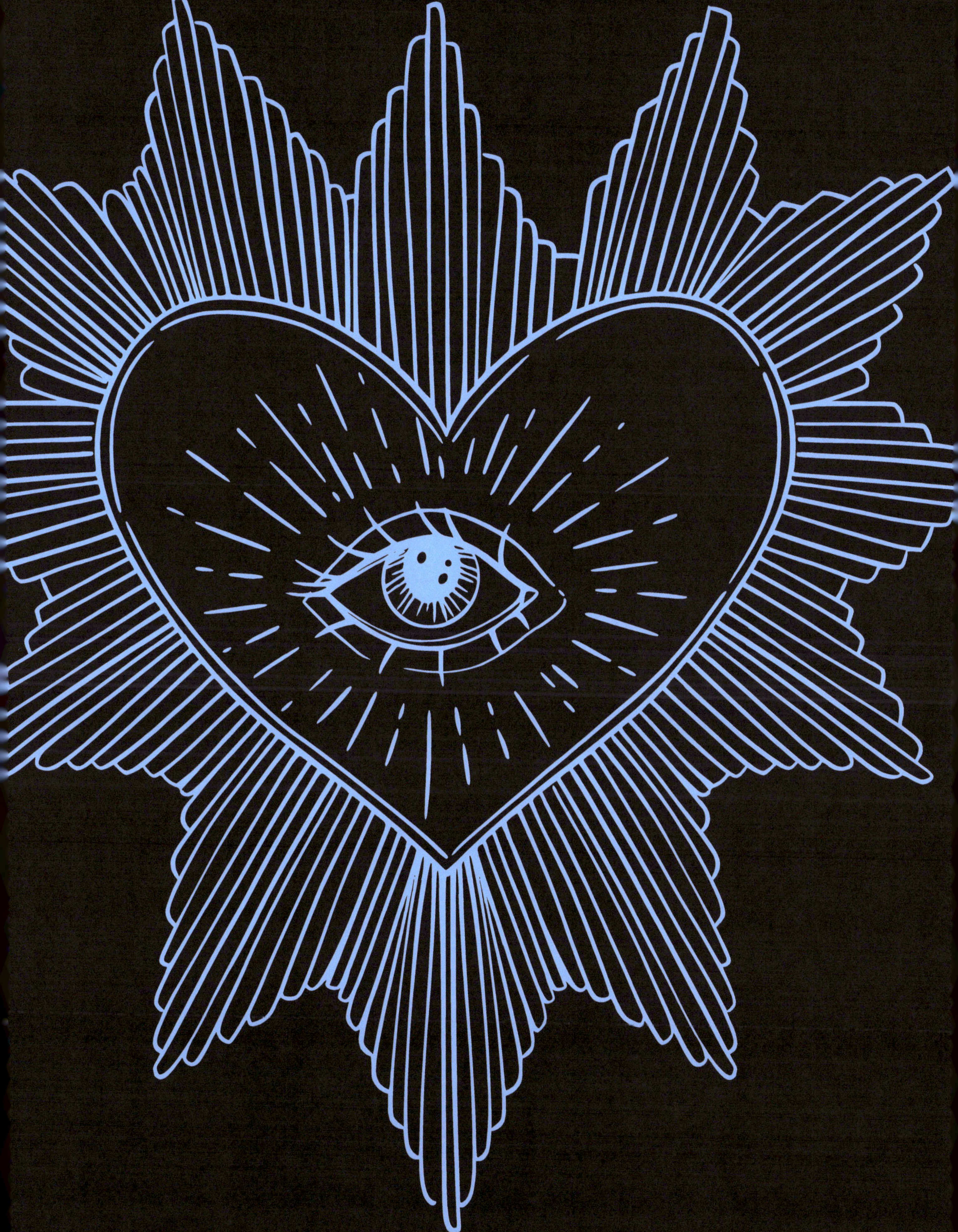

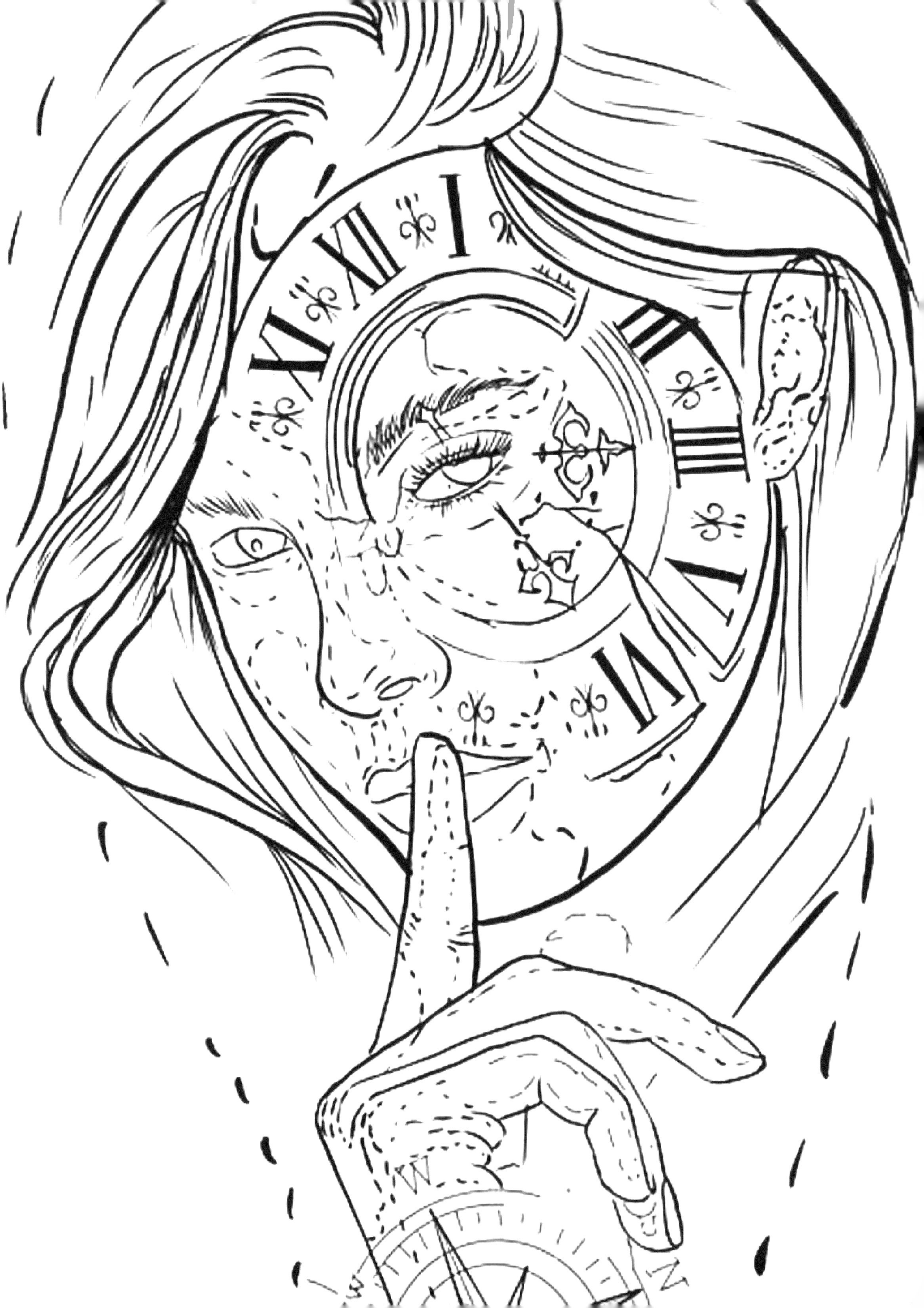

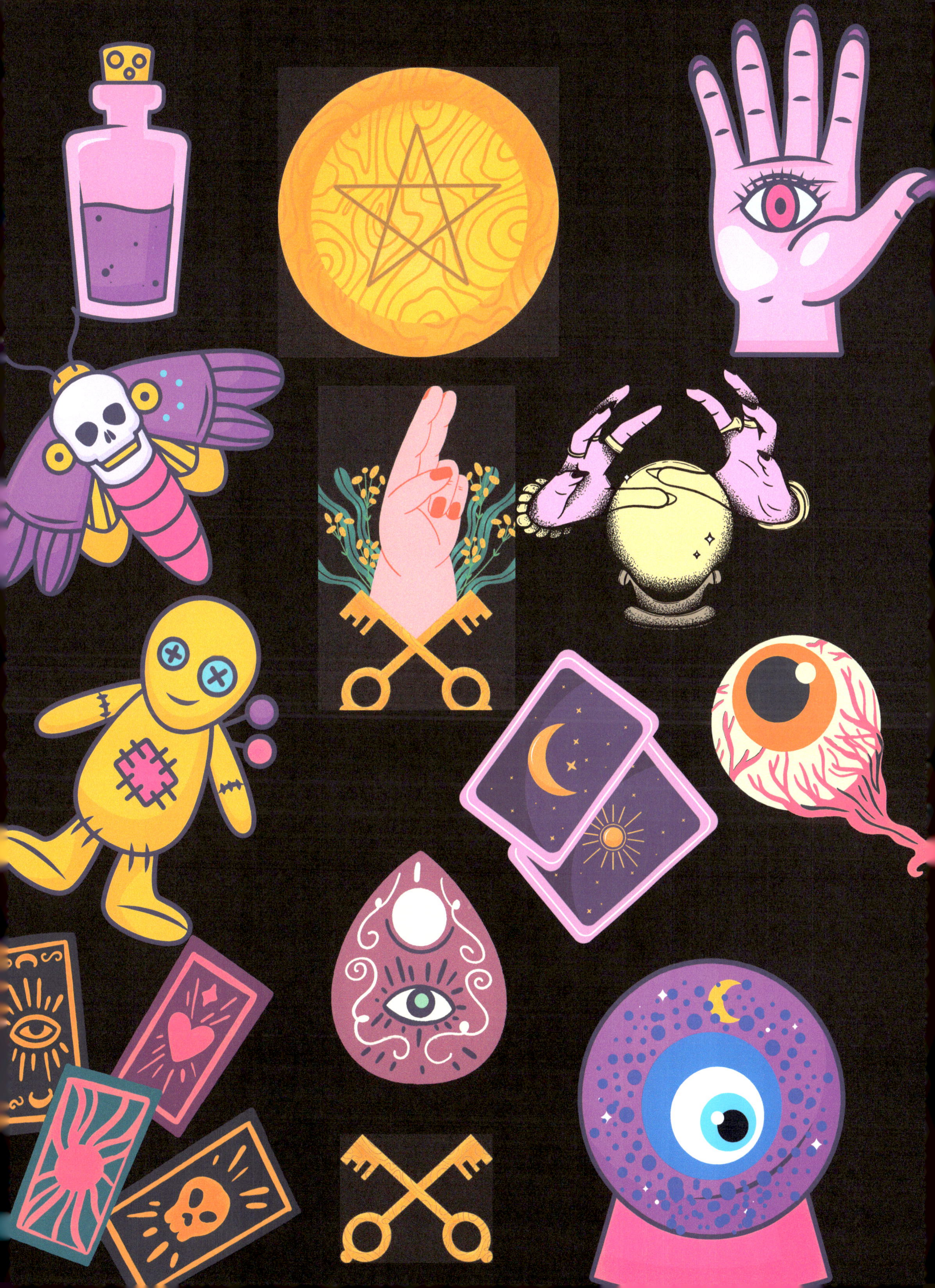

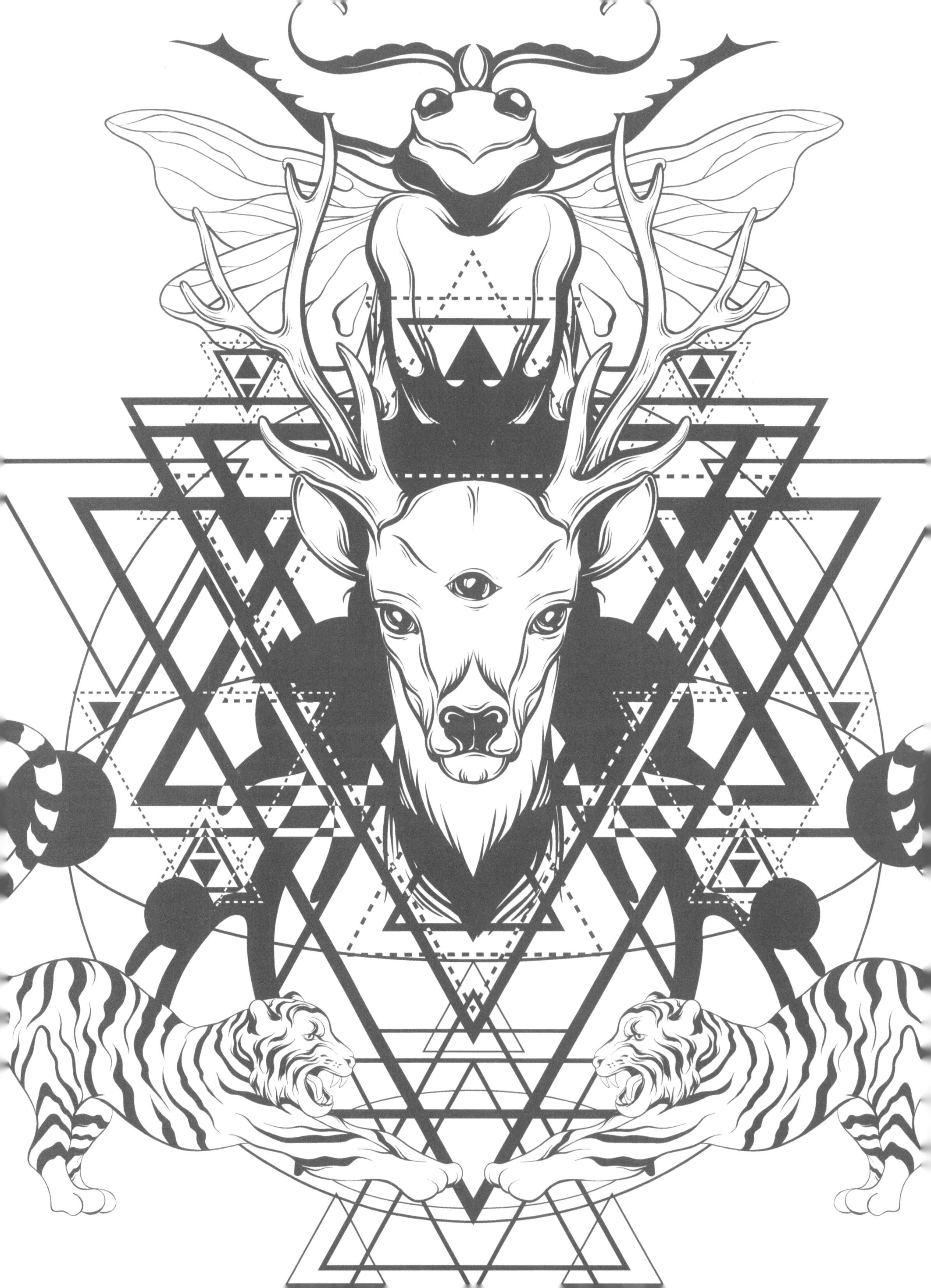

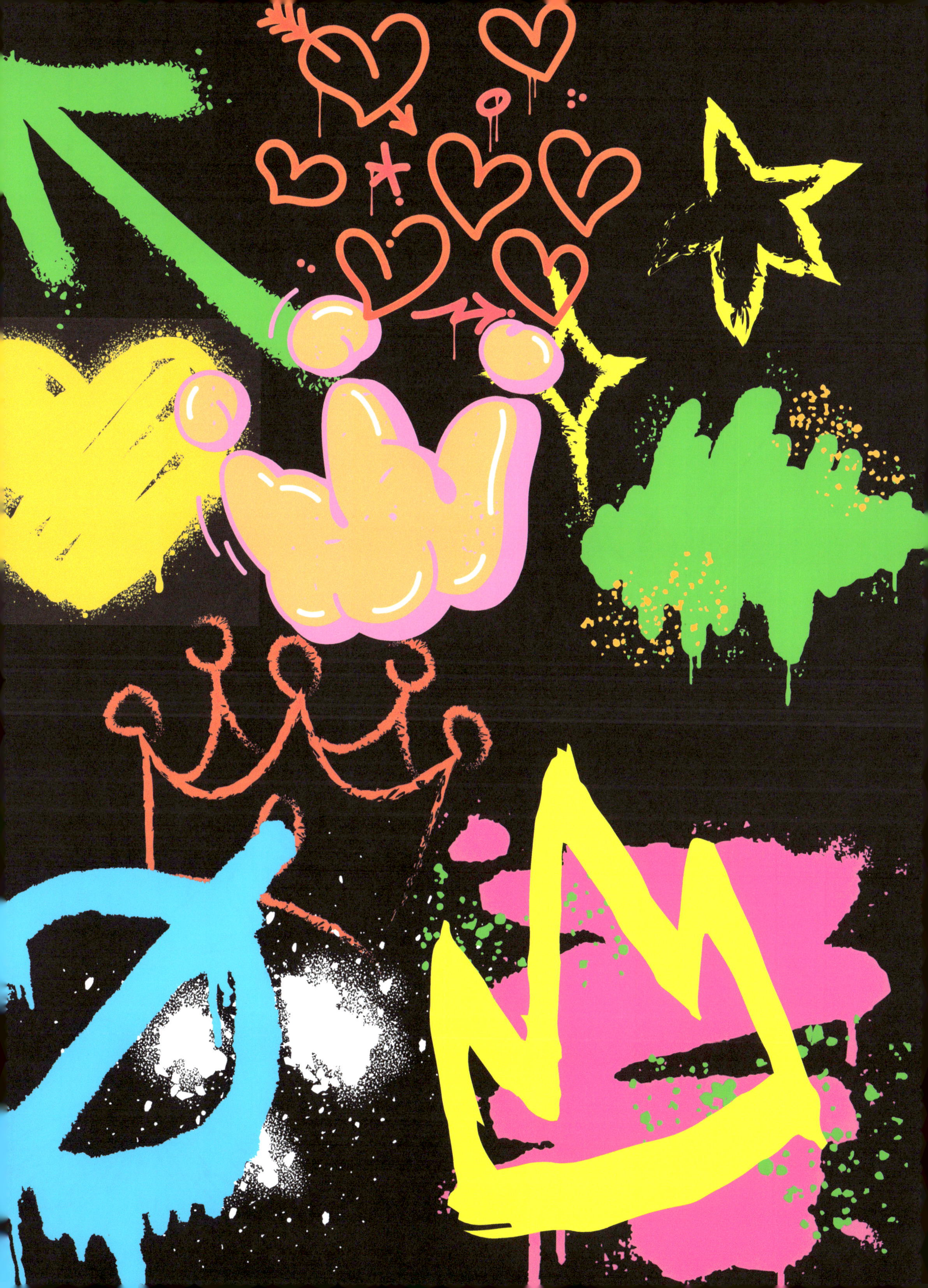

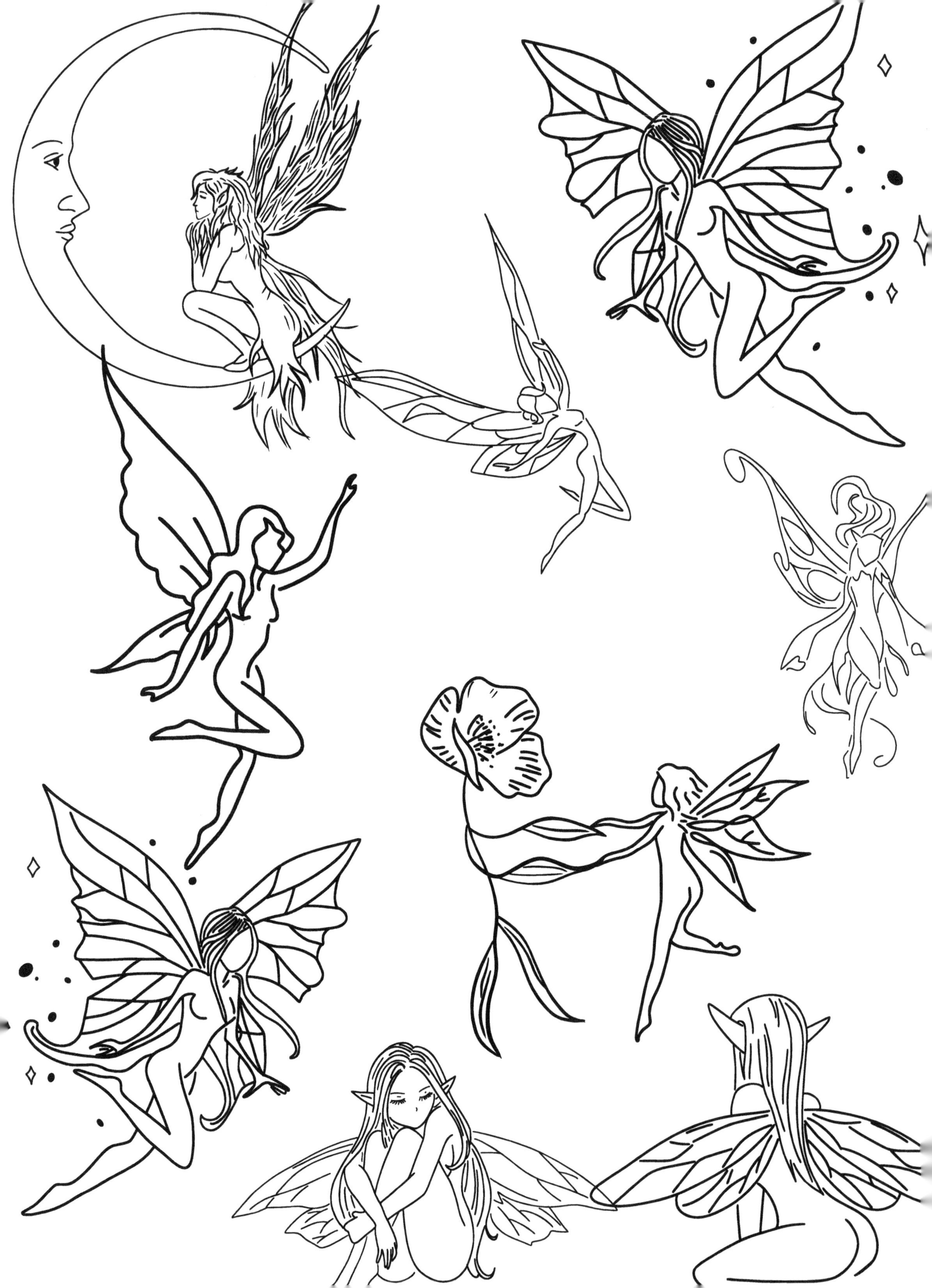

www.ingramcontent.com/pod-product-compliance
Lightning Source LLC
Chambersburg PA
CBHW041933240526
45473CB00034B/949
9798351349244